To Adkibi
from Artrella

COULD HAVE, SHOULD HAVE, WOULD HAVE

A journey from self-deprivation to self-acceptance

http://www.artrella.org

This book is dedicated to everyone who is going through or has gone through life's challenges, and has struggled to find workable solutions for conflicts in their life. It is for everyone who has reached a point in life when you want the pain to stop and you want to have peace within yourself.

"You can conquer others with power, but it takes true strength to conquer yourself." Lao Tzu

CONTENTS

INTRODUCTION

Do you fear losing relationships with significant others? Do you fear relationships with significant others are beyond repair? Are you tired of feeling disgusted, fearful, and anxious in the presence of those closest to you? Are you tired of feeling internal pain and inner conflict as you try to make sense of relationships between you and your significant others? Do you feel like screaming at the top of your lungs *I am sick of how you treat me and tired of dealing with you*? If you answered "yes" to any of these questions, this book is for you.

As a child, I lived in a torturous, fearful state, partly because of the constant adult battles within the family, and partly because of the torment inflicted upon me by these same adults. As an adult, whenever I saw two people in heated debate, I felt transported back to those angry scenes of my childhood and I would shake uncontrollably. I bore this fear most of my adult life and tried to avoid arguments at all costs, since they seemed too close to those memories.

Even though fear played a role in every facet of my life, I always felt there was an expiration date attached to anything that made me feel bad. Back then, when I was being punished or beaten for some rule or infraction, I would say to myself, *one day I am going to be an adult and these beatings and punishments will be over*. Repeating this to myself always comforted me when the punishment stopped and my body smarted with pain. Later in life, during difficult situations, my favorite words became, "this too shall pass."

Growing up, my self-esteem took quite a beating as I silently suffered hurts and injustices. After reaching adulthood, whenever pain became too unbearable, I sought solace by going into my bedroom, and behind closed doors, spoke my mind to the walls.

8

While this did not rectify the situation, it did help me connect with my inner-self and find some relief in "could have", "should have", or "would have" scenarios. Later in life, I realized that "could have", "should have", and "would have" thought patterns are in direct opposition to my growth. Their only function is to keep me bound to the past through shame, guilt, regret, anger, and confusion.

Through life's challenges, I have now reached a point in my life where I understand that everything, and I do mean everything, that has happened to me has served to make me a better and stronger person. Every fear and struggle I have experienced introduced me to parts of myself that I didn't know existed. The fear that once incapacitated me no longer strangles me into inactivity. I no longer suffer because of someone else's opinion of me. I no longer live in regret about what could have, should have, or would have happened if circumstances had been different. I no longer feel anxious about relationships or fear losing significant others. I no longer feel inner conflict about any relationship in my life. Best of all, I now trust myself enough to know what's right for me because, if it doesn't feel right to me, it ain't right for me.

ONCE YOU HAVE HAD ENOUGH

The other day as I sat a rocking; old thoughts came a knocking

Vying for my attention you see; forcing me to remember old hurts and things done to me

Remember when, they start; as my emotions begin to tear me apart

Push, push, tug, tug; any good feelings I had are now squashed like I crush bugs

My joyous feelings have gone astray; while bad ones linger and stay, and stay

So I begin to shout, hey emotions no way; you're not allowed to taunt me so just go away;

I ponder and wonder; cry and moan

I think I am the only one who feels so alone

Deeper and deeper inside me thoughts try to entrench themselves;

Woe is me I shout, thoughts return to my mind's shelf

But they linger and persist as if to say; hah, you thought you could get away

I'm stronger than you I begin to shout; my mouth forms a pout

So in an entreating way; I decide to pray

For I know fully; some thoughts are just bullies

They have no power you see; but if you let them be

They'll make you pay by ruining your day; while putting your mind in disarray

So if bad thoughts come a knocking; whether you're sitting or rocking

Just rear back and say "thought I'll give you no play"

Get out, get lost, just go away

Jesus lives here today

In the midst of healing my inner pain, I wrote this poem and read it often as a reminder to take stock of the situation and change my attitude. What I learned over time is that I do not have to walk around feeling so wounded and full of despair, even though my life no longer makes sense to me. I do not have to live under the domination of emotional baggage (anger, regret, shame, guilt, despair, frustration, just to name a few). I do not have to let negative thoughts play havoc with my life or continue to suffer at the hand of another human being. I realize now that perhaps I can't heal the situation between the offending individual and myself or situation being experienced, but I can take stock of my own state of mind and change unwanted, emotion-driven behavior. I can acknowledge my humanness by understanding that, as a human being, I am prone to make mistakes, which can be self-forgiven.

My tears of emotional angst about relationships in my life stopped the day I had an epiphany involving my second child. Some of my most unproductive and devastating emotions involved my relationship with my second offspring (more about this later). At best, our relationship was non-existent and, at worst, it was callous. There had been many episodes of crying out of frustration and anger, and sometimes out of a deep sense of loss. You know, it's the kind of anger and frustration you feel when you have been taken advantage of and can do nothing about it, the kind of loss you feel when you no longer have someone or something you once had or thought you had. But healing began the day my tears were interrupted by an epiphany in which I realized I am a victim of my own emotions and to circumstances beyond my control.

Clarity about the relationship between my daughter and I happened during one of the rare times I allowed myself to sit at my bedroom window in the middle of the day, content to watch clouds roll by. I usually avoided spending time in this manner because unwanted thoughts invaded my conscious mind, accompanied by tears, which always managed to crash through my resolve "to cry no more". All of a sudden, while watching the cloud formations, I realized I had done everything humanly possible to have a relationship with this offspring, but to no avail. I felt like hurtful emotions of anger, regret, self-pity and frustration, just to name a few, had been replaced by clarity and calmness. I delved further into my emotions and realized I had accepted habitual, misery-causing thoughts as a valid way of thinking or feeling. I began to understand that dwelling on what could, should, and would have been only served to make me miserable and unhappy.

From then on, I questioned myself on the validity of any emotional angst I felt. Sometimes the answer was clear, sometimes not so clear, but I knew in order to be free of my constant companion of inner turmoil, a new line of thinking was in order. So I developed a new motto. From that time forward, whenever thoughts came up about what could have, should have, or would have been done in a situation, I countered them with, "*I choose not to allow this emotion I am experiencing to put me in a head tail spin because I am no longer a victim of anyone or anything I encounter.*"

After reaching adulthood, I handled life situations in a way I thought was in perfect harmony with who I was. Situations arose and re-arose, causing me to react in the same manner each time and experience the same amount of pain or disillusionment I had during the initial experience. My only relief from the internal pain I was feeling was to go down memory lane and relive the actions of an offender or relive an offending circumstance. In my mind, I would always come up with ways to make the offender pay for his or her offense, or I imagined how the situation should have happened differently. I would say things like: "This or that should not have happened because she/he should do this or that", "this or that would not have happened this way if she/he would have done this or that", and "I would not be experiencing this turmoil if he/she would do things differently". Sound familiar?

I spent hours and sometimes days and weeks lamenting about how a situation should be different until I reached a point of tolerable pain. Once I reached my tolerable pain point in which the pain became a dull ache, I either pushed the pain deeper inside myself or let if fester while I created a craft or made an outfit. Either way, I chose to deal with the situation. The hurt remained and would resurface the minute a similar situation confronted me. I did not realize the extent of my self-inflicted misery until many tears later.

Have you ever found yourself living day-to-day on an emotional seesaw? It feels as though you make peace with something one minute and return to anger or whatever emotion you were feeling the next. I have, many times. What happens is two polar opposite emotions take turns activating and releasing each other. Some call this a crazy eight pattern. You find yourself in a crazy eight or seesaw pattern when you repeatedly ask yourself the same question, such as "why", or when you go straight into a mood that continuously returns, such as frustration. When you get tired of asking yourself why or feeling frustrated, another equally powerful emotion erupts, like sadness or anger.

It took me quite some time to fully understand the emotional seesaw or crazy eight pattern I was experiencing. I was unable to come to terms with the pattern until I exhausted every available avenue I could think of to reach out to my second born child. Once I became aware of this pattern, it was very clear to me that I had to leave a pain-driven situation in order to have peace of mind, to become the best that I was meant to be. I realized there is no shame, guilt, or regret associated with letting go of anything when you have given all you had to give and have forgiven yourself and the other party. When involved with others, if you find yourself teeter tottering between two extreme emotions, just remember being involved with another does not require you to live in pain or emotional turmoil. Give yourself permission to release yourself from the emotional pain because it really is freeing to do so.

There's an old saying: "If the shoe don't fit, don't wear it." This saying fits the relationship between my daughter and me quite well. I have come to understand that, when a relationship becomes estranged to a point where you can't find a way to make it work, you need to release it in order to release the pain.

As a child, I often overheard adults say, "child, if I knew what I know now I could have, should have, or would have…" They always finished the sentence with some kind of regret about something left undone or not accomplished. The sadness I saw in their faces made no sense to me. In silence, I would always pose the question, "Why couldn't you do what you wished you could do?" It never dawned on me that circumstances would prevent anyone from doing something they vehemently wanted to do. Yet, on numerous occasions as an adult, I sat in the same state of sadness I witnessed as a child.

It horrified me to realize I was in a vicious cycle of regret centering around could have, should have, and would have. The maelstrom of emotions (anger, fear, sorrow, despair and hurt) vibrating inside me awakened what I called my "personal demons". Each demon: defeat, uncertainty, dis-ease, regret, anger and self-pity interrupted my natural inclination to accept what I felt was an unchangeable situation. A part of me wanted to move forward and forget I had a daughter, while another part of me wanted to have a relationship with her.

My demons would win, because I would recount all the times I tried to maintain a relationship with my daughter only to be hurt in some way. I could not move beyond feeling self-righteous indignation for being placed in the position of wanting what obviously did not want me. After years of torment, I was able to refocus my thinking and accept there was another way of looking at the relationship between my daughter and me.

This new way of thinking came about through quite reflection during which I asked myself, "What could have caused such an enormous rift between my daughter and I? How can the rift be fixed?" The answer I received was, "You cannot become a doormat for this person to use and abuse. Whatever your daughter dishes out to you will return to her through her own life experiences. Karma always returns to its source. Just turn the situation over to God and let it go." These insights eased the emotional dross I was feeling and provided me with relief from negative emotions.

"All my life I had to fight. I had to fight my daddy. I had to fight my uncles. I had to fight my brothers. A girl child ain't safe in a family of men, but I ain't never thought I'd have to fight in my own house! I love Harpo, God knows I do. But I'll kill him dead before I let him beat me." Sofia in *The Color Purple*

Sometimes we come across words that parallel our life and, in so doing, provide an impetus to overcome the obstacles we face. These lines from the *Color Purple* have that effect on me. From the moment I first heard them spoken by Sofia to Miss Celie, they captivated me. These words inspire me to take one step at a time, to search for something that will gear my thinking to a more positive approach, and to hang in there and not let a situation get the better of me.

As a child, I lived in constant fear and confusion. As an adult, the constant challenge of balancing my needs with the needs of my family often resulted in inner turmoil and a fear of being perceived as weak. As I grew older, and as a way of self-protection, I paraphrased Sofia's lines to:

All my life I had to mentally fight. I had to fight my guardian, I had to fight my feelings of inferiority, I had to fight to keep from

15

becoming full of despair or dysfunctional, I had to balance my need for security and love against the need of my guardian to control me. And later, the needs of my offspring. A sensitive spirit ain't safe in the throes of tyrannical behavior from significant others. I love my guardian and children, God knows I do. But I will cut off all ties with them before I allow them to conquer my spirit.

Somehow paraphrasing these lines encouraged me to keep going, and sometimes the lines made me laugh. Whichever way I felt, encouraged or amused, a feeling of hope and triumph replaced any feelings I had of desolation and despair.

YOU CAN ONLY TEACH WHAT YOU HAVE LEARNED

It never dawned on me until much later in life that the way we interact with others, unless we have made a conscious effort to weed out anything that no longer serves us in a beneficial way, is a direct result of the things we were taught. My foster mother taught me many things, whether I wanted to learn them or not. She taught me about work ethic and honesty, that it was okay to care about my fellow humans, and countless other principles and traits. I may not have agreed with her methods of teaching, but now I think of her with gratitude because she raised me to the best of her ability. She taught me all she knew. I no longer see her as the enemy, but as a person who took on the responsibilities of raising me while suffering through her own challenges. I want to share her story with you.

I cannot tell my story without first telling the story of my foster mother, Calee, and her sister, Mae. Their upbringing had a direct impact on my life because of the disciplinary methods used in training me as well as the morals and values they passed down to me from their own childhood. Calee was born in either 1908 or 1910 and was raised in the Deep South. In the dead of winter, her mother dropped her and Mae on their father's doorstep with nothing but the clothes on their back, and left town.

Calee was five years old. Her sister was three. For her entire life, Calee felt the pain of being abandoned. Whenever she talked about it, she would shed tears as she vividly recalled the bitterly cold temperature and how she and her sister had to huddle together to keep warm, how scared and hungry they were, and how dark it was before their father arrived. Her childhood consisted of picking cotton, obeying her father's rules, doing all of the household chores, and learning to cook and sew while being responsible for her younger sister. Her father, a sharecropper whom she lovingly called papa was a short, medium-built man who, year round, wore two pairs of pants held up by suspenders. He was not affectionate with his children. He had one other living relative, a brother, and was a hard worker with a quick temper. Mr. Charlie, a white man who owned the land that papa worked, was very kind to the family and Calee always praised him as being a good person who helped the family whenever they needed help.

I never thought much of papa because of the incident Calee recalled when she was a child. After living with Papa for a while, she was told to comb her hair. For some reason, she never got around to combing her hair and after the third time, papa picked up a rake laying nearby, put her in a thigh grip that was impossible for her to squirm out of, and combed her hair with it while disregarding her tears and pleas. She would always end the story with, "I combed my hair from then on." I always felt this was cruel and abusive, so I developed a dislike of papa. Calee quit school after the third grade and she only knew how to sign her name with an "x." I'm told by relatives that Calee always stood up for her beliefs, and if cornered, would fight as ferociously as necessary to win the battle (this seems pretty accurate to me, because every relative I ever met would only challenge Calee so far before stopping). On the other hand, if you needed help, she was right there.

At fourteen, Calee married a man called Miss Tommy. He was 14 years older than she was, tall, and always maintained a job. She always said he robbed the cradle when he married her. They soon became parents of twin boys who later died as infants. She always seemed to grieve over the loss of the twins and it seemed, at times, that her biological daughter and I played second fiddle to their memory. Lucy, her third and only living child, was born some years later.

While working at a bar, Calee and another woman got in an argument. A knife fight ensued. Calee severely injured her opponent so she went into hiding. While in hiding, a friend told Calee the person she had cut so badly was looking to exact revenge by shooting her to death. Prudency outweighed her resolve to remain in the area. She got as much money together as she could and fled town, temporarily leaving behind her husband and child.

After arriving in Washington, D.C., she stayed with my great aunt until she could find employment with the railroad and send for her child. Miss Tommy followed and found work as a trash collector with the city. Soon they were able to purchase a home and vehicle.

Miss Tommy and Calee's marriage was wrought with constant battles, both verbally and physically. In the beginning, my anger at Calee for the way she treated me meant I usually rooted for Miss Tommy to win, but then I'd root for Calee if she seemed to be losing the fight. Their battles always left me shaken and in desperate need of a respite from the drama happening right before my eyes. Having nowhere to go and wait out the storm, I could only stare in horror and tremble in fear while the two of them battled each other to see who could inflict the most physical pain. No matter who I rooted for, I always felt fearful the two of them would destroy each other. I felt anger towards both of them for fighting with each other. A visit from the police usually ended their fight, although they would continue flinging verbal insults at each other for a while afterward. Even after the altercation was over and the two of them were civil to each other, I was afraid they were going to seriously hurt or kill each other. This feeling of immobilized fear continued to be part of my personality well into adulthood whenever I witnessed people in a heated argument. Later, I referred to this fear as one of my demons because of its intensity and longevity in my life.

Calee's closest relative was Mae, the baby sister she helped raise. Aunt Mae moved to Washington, D.C. with her husband and three children at Calee's urging. The fights between adults in Aunt Mae's home always resulted in hostility between all of the household members. I used to think this must be what a war was like. The oldest of Aunt Mae's children, Jab, was always asking for handouts from his parents and Calee. He, his wife, and eight children lived rent-free in the tiny, single room basement of his parent's home. Not only did he and his family's living arrangement seem normal to me, but the harsh way he talked to his parents when he wasn't cussing them out stupefied me. I knew I had better not attempt to talk in such a manner to Calee, so I was confused as to why this behavior was tolerated by Aunt Mae and her husband, Uncle G.

Aunt Mae's middle child was a girl whose boyfriends frequently and severely beat her. Whenever Mink visited her parents, she always had either a broken arm, black eyes, busted lips, a broken jaw, or broken leg. Her constant trips to a medical facility appeared to hold no purpose other than to wear her bruises and breaks as badges of courage. I never understood why Mink allowed herself to be another's punching bag. I could not look at Mink without feeling angry with her for allowing herself to be treated in this way.

Aunt Mae's youngest child was called Dink. Unlike his older siblings, Dink worked odd jobs long enough to get money for his booze binges. Whenever I was around him, I stared at him on edge as he drank until he turned into an insulting, staggering drunk. I watched Dink bump into walls, fall down, start fights, and get beat up. The drunken stench of him was nauseating. He was put in the hospital quite a few times because of DTs, an illness called "delirium tremens" that is associated with alcohol withdrawal.

My observation of both Mink and Dink taught me that drunken individuals experience the world through rage and pain. I always felt Aunt Mae's family should have been better people, and because they were not who I wanted them to be, I felt disdain and anger towards them. Could have, should have, and would have always dominated any thoughts I had about Aunt Mae and Uncle G's family. I thought the family could have been nicer to each other, but they weren't. I thought the family should have tried to be more tolerant of each other, but they couldn't or wouldn't. I thought they would have a calmer home if they listened to each other before an argument erupted, but that was never the case. The most important lessons I learned from Aunt Mae's family was that I should not allow myself to become a man's punching bag or stay in an intolerable situation longer than necessary.

I used to blame others for making me feel bad. I especially blamed relatives for not being who I wanted them to be. I always felt everyone should be, do, and act the way I wanted them to, and when this did not happen, I blamed them for the anger I felt towards them.

I have since learned the following: *"All blame is a waste of time. No matter how much fault you find with another, and regardless of how much you blame them, it will not change you. The only thing blame does is keep the focus off of you because you are looking for external reasons to explain your unhappiness or frustration. You may succeed in making another feel guilty about something by blaming them, but you won't succeed in changing whatever it is about you that is making you unhappy."* Dr. Wayne Dyer

Desperate

I just want to crawl into a corner; And wail like a mourner

I am too tired to run; Even though life is no fun

I am too tired to groan; so I sit and just inwardly moan

I don't want to think; maybe I should just have a drink, but instead

I crawl into a corner; and wail like a mourner

I smile on the outside, I cry on the in

Again and again I pray Lord when, oh when, will it end

Nothing changes so I just crawl into a corner; And wail like a mourner

When I stare at a mountain; or squint at a road

I try to balance life's heavy load

Many visions of triumph and heartache appear

But I no longer want to see or hear

I only want to crawl into a corner and wail as a mourner

I can't get mad there's no energy left; I used it all up while crying and feeling bereft

Make lemonade is what others say when life deals you sour lemons in every way

Get back sour lemons I shout, leave me alone go away and don't come back any more today

Still those old sour lemons come in one form or another

Taunting and teasing me as if to say; you will never get away

So I just crawl into a corner; and continue to wail like a mourner

THE BEGINNING OF COULD HAVE, SHOULD HAVE, WOULD HAVE

My childhood began like that of so many others. An unwed mother gave me birth and then decided to put me in foster care. Not much was known about my father except his first name. According to my great aunt, he was incarcerated after he robbed a store on his way to visit me. I became a ward of a third cousin, Calee, and grew up feeling starved for affection: unloved, alienated, yet somehow connected emotionally to this third cousin who raised me. I tried hard to believe there must have been a logical reason my biological mother gave me up for adoption, even though Calee often told me that segment of the family was "no god damn good." I sometimes got very angry with Calee for the remarks she made about my biological family. I wondered who gave her the right to speak in such harsh terms about my biological mother and family members. I could not show my anger because to do so meant enduring physical pain. It might come in the form of a slap across the face or a whipping with a switch or electrical cord, so I remained silent and stoic.

Calee often reminded me that my biological mother gave birth to me and another boy child out of wedlock. She gave us both up, got married, and had three more children who she raised in her home. Sometimes I felt confused and torn between wanting to accept that my mother was "no god damn good," and my need to feel there was a good reason I was not with her. I finally concluded, after hearing numerous times "them damn people ain't no good," that Calee was the one keeping my biological mother and I apart. Adopting the belief that Calee was keeping my mother and I apart helped me create a place inside that could not be touched by Calee or her family-bashing tirades.

I grew up in the suburbs of Washington, D.C. There were only four houses on my street and each house had two parents and at least one kid. I had no concept of racism because I was never allowed to venture outside of my neighborhood unescorted. Every person in my neighborhood, including shopkeepers, a doctor, a lawyer, and some of the people I saw on T.V. were the same color as me. I assumed white people were good people because Calee always talked in glowing terms about a white man named Mr. Charlie who had befriended her and her family whenever she needed assistance. The only time I came close to racism was during a road trip to visit relatives in Ohio. We stopped at a gas station and I noticed two signs. One read "white" and the other "colored". I asked Calee what the signs meant. She promptly thanked me for pointing them out and said, "It means we cannot use that bathroom." We found and used the other bathroom designated "colored" and went on our way. The experience confused me, but did not completely alter my opinion that people could be kind and generous, regardless of color.

For the most part, my childhood felt lonely and set apart from everyone around me. I was not permitted to show or demonstrate emotions openly to anyone or to be in the company of anyone deemed "no damned good" by Calee. I vacillated between the emotional extremes of anger, sadness, and the yearning to feel acceptable in the eyes of my family. This yearning for acceptance built up an overwhelming feeling of isolation. I felt unloved and unlovable, as if I was drowning in the fear of being rejected.

I also lived in constant fear of being beaten. Invariably, I was the depository of Calee's anger which came in the form of tongue lashings, slaps, being hit with whatever was nearby, or beaten with an extension cord or tree branch called a switch. I could never come to terms with the idea that the harsh and critical tongue-lashings and beatings came from a person I considered to be a tyrannical bully, but who was also the person that made sure that my needs were met.

Being a kid in my house meant you were seen and not heard. You did whatever tasks you were given to do without showing any sign of complaint. You didn't look at any adult in any way that could be misconstrued as confrontational. You said "yes sir", "no sir", and "yes ma'am" and "no ma'am". You came in from the outside at dark. You did not dispute what any adult said and whatever your parent said was the law, no questions asked. You only played in your own back yard and seldom with other kids. Break any of these rules and the result was a beating, and you didn't get a warning not to do it again, either.

My only relief from the everyday experiences of my childhood came from the imaginary world I created. In my imaginary world, I felt as though I had value and purpose because I usually felt lonely, fearful, and awkward around others. My favorite way of amusing myself was to create scenarios using dolls that I fashioned from sticks, old rags, and cording. My preferred way to play was to pretend the dolls came to me needing help with a problem. I would help my creations with their problem, create new clothing for them, and send them on their way to a nice evening gala or dinner. These imaginary playmates were the highlight of my childhood and the scenarios I imagined while playing with them afforded me a time of reprieve from my own living experience. This was my beginning of could have, should have, and would have.

Calee would often ask me why I couldn't be more like her biological daughter. "She never gives me any trouble" (of course, she never talked about the big arguments they had and that her biological daughter was 20 years older than I was). Right behind those words came, "I guess you just gone be like them damn, no good peoples." Those last words didn't have the effect she apparently intended them to have on me, since the only no good people I knew was my great aunt, and I liked her.

I internalized Calee's constant disapproval of me to mean I was not an acceptable human being under any circumstances. This feeling culminated in me spending years of my adult life trying to prove I deserved to be loved and wanted. I had numerous sexual liaisons. I learned how to make crafts and gave these things I had made away just so the person would think well of me and pay me a compliment. Giving away my creations had the effect of showing me I had done something of value, that my life was worthwhile and good, and that I was appreciated.

I wanted so desperately to feel love from Calee (a hug, a kind word, something) but all I felt was an unfulfilled ache inside. The ache climaxed over time into a feeling that I was alien. When I grew older, I even nicknamed myself "space alien" because I found it difficult to express my feelings and feel accepted by others. Mentally, I felt as though I was a different species from anyone around me. I had no sense of being a part of anyone and my only solace came from playing with the stick dolls I created. Nobody ever seemed to show me loving kindness or teach me in a loving way, so I suffered internally, yet I lived in hope that someday, in some way, someone would show me they cared about me.

In trying to figure out a way to avoid being insulted or hurt by Calee, I hatched a plan to become the perfect child. I believed being a perfect child would make her happy and that I would become a more acceptable human being in her eyes. So I set out doing everything exactly as I was told. I volunteered to do extra chores around the house and ran to the store as often as asked without complaint, which was usually twice while a meal was being prepared. I stuck close by so I could immediately respond to her every command. After a week of being Miss Perfect, I found nothing had changed. I was still the object of her disapproval and ire, so I reverted to my old self of suffering her insults in silence, tolerating her beatings while loathing my situation.

One day I sensed Calee was in a lot of pain, and seeing the sadness in her eyes was more than I could bear. All I wanted to do was help ease her pain so she would feel better, so I called her "ma" in hopes she would realize I was there for her. Bad move on my part. She snapped at me, "don't call me "ma". I ain't your god damn mammy." I felt deeply hurt, confused, rejected, fearful, lost, and alone because I had always considered her my surrogate mother, even though I felt she was a tyrant.

I did not understand why she was so angry with me and I began to ask myself fearful questions. Was she throwing me out of her house? If so, why? Why did she not want to be my mother? If she were not my mother then who was she to me and I to her, and why was I living in her house? Unable to come up with an answer to my questions, I internalized the pain to mean I was not worthy as a human being.

My anger and resentment towards Calee began to kick into gear and nothing was ever the same between us after that. My life took on new meaning because I realized I had a mind of my own and I stopped wanting Calee to show me love. I felt as though an empty space had been created inside me that I didn't know how to fill. My yearning for acceptance and love was replaced with apathy. I started running away from home and deliberately doing things I knew I would be punished for because I no longer cared about the consequences of my actions.

One of the most devastating things Calee used to say to me after a meal was, "God bless the cook and god damn the dishwasher." Of course, I was the dishwasher. Calee's words, coupled with her laughter, had the impact of making me feel unwanted, unimportant, and unloved. I could not reveal to Calee how her words affected me for fear of being ridiculed even more, or beaten, so I pushed the hurt down inside. Over time, my hurt feelings deepened and my anger began to turn into rage towards Calee.

My first recollection of feeling deep, impenetrable anger towards Calee happened when I was eight years old. I awoke one night filled with anger at the treatment I was receiving and I began to fantasize how to kill Calee. I envisioned getting out of bed, walking into the kitchen, grabbing a big butcher knife, walking into the bedroom she shared with Miss Tommy and, using the knife as a saw, cutting off her head. The only reason I didn't follow through with that fantasy was that I knew Miss Tommy was asleep next to her. I felt that he would probably stop me from carrying out the act, and I wasn't sure I could get rid of him in the same manner before he had a chance to stop me. I wasn't scared of receiving repercussions from the violent act I was fantasizing about because I had concocted a story in my mind of what I was going to tell the police. I would tell them I had awakened to a frightening noise and was too afraid to investigate until the house became quiet, and that I found the two of them in this condition, and that was why I had blood on my nightgown.

After realizing my plan was unworkable, I ran away from home a short time afterwards. The adults claimed there was no apparent reason for my actions and I could not explain them either at that time, but when I was away from Calee, I felt free and alive and more like a human being, instead of like a herded cow that needs prodding and whipping at the least provocation. Uppermost in my mind was that this lady I had to live with was mean, spiteful, and hateful, and I just wanted to be free of her.

Expressing my feelings was not permitted when I was growing up, so I engaged in mental fights with my tormentors. Inside me seethed a cauldron of anger and frustration from the constant and unjust punishments, so whenever I reached a point where I could not stand being tormented a moment longer, I ran away.

I vividly remember the first time I ran away. I had gotten out of school and was on my way to Aunt Mae's house. In the beginning, I did not mind going to Aunt Mae's because her grandchildren and I were playmates and I felt somewhat free from the constant consternation of adults.

After Aunt Mae's grandchildren were no longer living with her, I felt lonesome, in need of companionship, and I no longer enjoyed going to her house after school. The constant bickering between Aunt Mae and her adult children used to leave me shaking and in fear that someone was going to be seriously hurt. One day after school, I saw my chance for a reprieve from adult bickering and supervision. I saw some children playing and I could not resist

29

joining in on the fun. It was one of those times I felt like making a choice for myself without caring about the consequences. It felt wonderful to feel accepted by others. As dark was approaching and I saw Calee's car slowly coming up the street, I panicked and realized I was in big trouble. I knew my evening was going to end with a whipping and tongue lashing, so in an instant, I decided that would not happen. I hid amongst the children I was playing with and, after dark when the children went to their respective homes, I was left having to make a decision about what to do next.

I had not thought about what to do beyond having a fun afternoon playing with other kids. I felt fearful and unsure about my next move. After some self-debate, I decided that even though I was really in for a long whipping, I should go home and face the music. The closer I got to my home, the less inclined I felt to go there. I began to feel petrified and decided I did not feel like being whipped. Spotting an apartment building, I decided to go inside and sleep there until the morning, thinking that maybe Calee would be cooled down enough not to hurt me too bad. Going inside of the apartment building, I spotted a red wagon on the basement level and decided to sleep in the wagon until morning. I was awakened by two adults, one male and one female, who insisted upon taking me home. Even though I pretended not to know where I lived, the two adults kept insisting I did and finally I relented and pointed them to my home. Once the two people left, I received an extension cord whipping and tongue lashing for my disobedience but, for the first time in my life, I felt the pain of the extension cord whipping and tongue-lashing was worth it.

My afternoon of play was only a short reprieve from what I considered an environment laden with hostility and rules, but running away from it gave me a new perspective on life. Being whipped for running away did not take away from my feeling of exhilaration in being free from the stranglehold of my tormentor, Calee. I was able to hold onto that exhilarated feeling of freedom for quite some time after the fervor of my running away had died down. From then on, whenever I received a whipping, I would release the pain by mentally returning to my afternoon of freedom and re-experiencing the joy I felt playing with the other children.

In my growing years, there were numerous beatings, which preceded the words "you know better than that." In actuality, I didn't know better most of time. Going to school, smarting from the visible welts on my body made me sad and, at times, very angry. Calee's threat of "I'm gone whip your ass" brought terror to my whole being, causing my body to tremble uncontrollably. I feared the pain of each blow to my body. I feared the smarting of the whelps left from the beating I received. I feared the tongue-lashing of how bad of a person I was. I feared the feeling of worthlessness I felt as a result of the tongue-lashing. When I turned seven years of age, I realized that whippings were an inevitable part of my life, no matter how good I tried to be. Once I gained this understanding, I began to develop a tolerance to the pain and sought a way to get through it.

Another reprieve from pain turned out to be the development of my sixth sense. Believing it was inevitable to have pain inflicted on my psyche and body, I needed a way to lessen the pain. Developing my sixth sense allowed me to turn my attention inward to a place Calee could not reach with her tongue-lashings, and allowed me to feel mentally untouched until the punishment was over. While this stance did not lessen the physical pain and humiliation of having my person assaulted, it did enhance my resolve to get to a point in life where Calee could never hit or hurt me again.

One of the few times I was allowed to go anywhere with another individual was the day I went on a church-sponsored beach trip with a neighbor's family. I was more elated about being free from Calee's stranglehold than the trip. While at the beach, a neighbor's son playfully ducked me under the water. As he tried to pull me back to the surface, I pulled against his tug, trying to decide whether to permanently remain under water and die or allow myself to be pulled back to the surface. I stayed under the water for what seemed like a long time while that poor, scared kid tried in vain to pull me back up to the surface. While under the water, I asked myself, "should I stay and drown, or allow myself to be pulled back up?" Suddenly, a voice inside my head said, "your choice." Feeling shaken and unsure of which was the best way to proceed, I gave up my quest for death and allowed myself to be pulled up to the surface of the water.

I was admonished by the kid who dunked me. He asked why I was trying to kill myself, telling me I really scared him, and that he wasn't going to play with me anymore. No matter how much I denied trying to kill myself, the poor kid would not believe me. After a few more admonishments about my inconsideration, he turned and walked away. I felt alone again, confused and heartbroken. Even though I was given a stern talking to about my actions, I somehow felt this person cared about my wellbeing, which made me reevaluate my suicidal thoughts. After careful consideration, I decided to let my death wish go and just deal with Calee's harshness the best that I could.

I HAVE NO SAFE HAVEN

The only two men I remember Calee being involved with certainly didn't benefit me. There wasn't much to say about Calee's husband, Miss Tommy, except that he molested me at an early age. I didn't tell Calee about the molestation until I became very angry with him. I don't remember why I became angry with him but, when I did, I was unable to stop thinking about how helpless I felt when he touched me. When I finally got the courage to reveal the molestation, a fight between Calee and Miss Tommy ensued and he was promptly barred from the house. Calee had me examined by the family doctor and was told that, since I was so small when the event occurred, I probably would not remember it and that there would be no permanent damage to me. The doctor was wrong. I did remember the incident many years later.

My life at the time was pretty mundane. My children were at an age of self-sufficiency, I was gainfully employed with the government, and I was enjoying dating again. I don't recall all the details, but I found myself in an out of body experience one afternoon. I had taken the day off from work and the kids were at school when I found myself looking down at a very young child lying in a crib with a man standing over her, manipulating her genitals with his fingers. I saw his body stiffen and his eyes roll back as if he was in a trance. I could not remove myself from what I was seeing. I could only stare at what was happening to the little, helpless creature being tortured by the man. I suddenly realized I was the little girl being molested and the man molesting me was Miss Tommy. As I watched, transfixed at the scene before me, I could feel the pressure of his fingers on my vagina. When he placed his other hand over my mouth I realized, to my horror, I was at his mercy. Leaning back, he pulled out his penis and placed its tip on the outside of my vagina, saying, "I better not put it in any further because someone will know." He put his penis back in his pants, and soon a woman appeared in the doorway, asking him what he was doing as she shooed him out of the room.

Seeing this vision and experiencing the pain of what had been done to me helped me understand why I never felt close to Miss Tommy, and why I always pretty much kept my distance from him. The only comfort from re-experiencing this was the tears that came then, hot and heavy, an outpouring that didn't stop for quite some time. Once they subsided, I was able to pull myself together. Though still confused, some small part of me felt as though I had healed a little.

The other love of Calee's life was named Charles. He was a real piece of work. They met on the job site, and once they grew close, he was allowed to move in. Because they had separate days off, Calee left me in his custody when she went to work, and there started my second experience with Calee's male loves. When she was around, he paid very little attention to me, but when she went to work, he pressured me endlessly for sex, offering false promises and threats. My breaking point came when I became angry with Calee for being nasty towards me. Charles picked up on this and began to pressure me even more for sex. He coerced me into having sex with him by threatening to tell Calee that I was getting fresh with him. He told me she would believe him because he was the adult. He added that she was going to beat the hell out of me for telling lies on him because he was the believable one, and with my track record of running away from home, she would believe him before me.

My sexual misfortune with Charles went on for a year or more. Since I was unable to tell Calee about what was going on with Charles, and because I couldn't take it anymore, I ran away from home again, only to be returned by the police. Yes, you guessed it. Another beating and tongue-lashing. To my relief and joy, Calee and Charles broke up soon after I was returned home, but the sadness in her eyes put a real damper on my exhilaration. It was as though she was going through the motions of living. She carried such a heaviness about her that I almost wished my nemesis, Charles, would return to the household so her sadness would be over. Eventually though, things returned to normal and I was, again, the object of her ire.

All physical beatings stopped when I was 13 years old. I got my first period at school one day and came home all excited and told Calee. The only reason I knew about menstruation was through class. It was explained as a natural part of life. To my surprise, she began pummeling me with her fist, repeating, "so you think you are a woman, so you think you grown." Over and over, she repeated these words as she punched and hit me. All of a sudden, a quiet, eerie feeling engulfed me and I stood up to my full height. As I looked at her, I no longer felt fear or the pain of her blows on my body. A deadly, quiet rage had replaced any fear I had. My thoughts turned from dodging her blows to knocking her to the floor. I abruptly knew that if she continued to hit me, I was going to retaliate by giving her a taste of her own medicine. I had reached a point of saturation. My mind began to focus on how best to hurt her, because I was not going to take another blow from her ever again. She must have seen my rage because she suddenly stopped hitting me and walked away. I stared at her retreating back as I tried to gain control of my emotions. I was unable to let go of my rage until Calee came back with torn sheets and showed me how to use them to block the flow of blood from reaching my underwear. I felt things had changed between us and I no longer felt threatened by her presence. Getting beat by Calee was finally over, to my relief.

ADOLESCENT DELIMMA

The last time I ran away from home was bad timing on my part. Calee got hurt on the railroad and, since she was unable to work or properly look after me, I was sent to Philadelphia to stay with Lucy, her biological daughter. I had always admired, revered, and considered Lucy my sister. Little did I know I was being sent to the residence of my archenemy.

During my childhood, I hardly saw Lucy, but when I did, she was always smiling, cheerful, and seemed to be a free spirit who had managed to survive Calee. I looked up to her and aspired to be like her. This opinion changed when I went to stay with her and discovered the real person was a bully, jealous, insecure, false, pretentious, and money hungry. Worst of all, I was stuck with her boyfriend, the sexually pestering church pastor. During the day, I was hounded by his promises to talk to Lucy and get her to leave me alone in exchange for my sexual favor. In the evening, I was the recipient of Lucy's tongue-lashings, which focused on how I wasn't much, that my lips were too big, and anything else she thought would tear me down. I did not understand why she often angrily looked at me saying, "you think you bad. I heard you think you are bad. Why don't you jump at me? C'mon, jump, jump at me." At first, I was petrified of her bullying ways, and the uncertainty of the outcome of her tirades. All I could do was deny that I thought I was bad and pray I didn't have to physically fight her. Even when she hit me, trying to make me hit her back, I could only look at her with hurt and dismay. All I wanted from her was love and acceptance; instead, I got harassed and goaded to fight. In the beginning, I was heartbroken and confused. I did not know what I could have done to make her treat me so wretchedly. Trying my best to stick it out, I withdrew into an imaginary world where I was an adult and living my life as I thought it could be.

Each Sunday, we went to church. While her boyfriend preached in the pulpit, sister dear sat looking and acting like a devout Christian. My hell would resume right after church. I could not understand why a church pastor and a church first lady could act so ungodly at home and so saintly in church. I lived in constant fear of being beaten up, and I worried about my reaction to the abuse I was receiving. Would I have to hurt the person I had always wanted to emulate? After a couple of weeks, I no longer looked up to her; instead I despised her. My resentment of the situation and Lucy's treatment of me grew to such an intolerable point, that I ran off again, even though I was in a strange city and knew no one.

Shortly after leaving Lucy's home, I was picked up in a park by a pimp who tried to make me a prostitute. He took me home with him, had my hair and makeup done, provided me an outfit, and told me if I couldn't perform sexually, he would drop me back off where he had found me. He cautioned me to follow his exact instructions, fulfill the needs of his customers, give him the money I received from them, and that I was to get no less than ten dollars for sex. I felt like I was in a daze and being led into something I didn't quite understand. We drove to an out of the way bar and I was told by the pimp to go with a man who had picked me out of a line-up of ladies the pimp brought along. Feeling unsure and nervous, I met the man and told him the price of my service was ten dollars. He said he only had seven dollars and fifty cents on him for oral sex. I refused his request, because at fifteen years of age, I had no idea how to perform oral sex. Besides, he didn't have enough money. When I told the pimp I didn't have sex with the guy because he didn't have all the money, he strode angrily to the customer I had refused. When he finished talking with the guy, he came back and told me to have sex with the guy and collect the seven dollars and fifty cents. I told the pimp I didn't know how to perform oral sex. He shot a look of exasperation at me and had one of the other ladies take care of the customer's sexual needs. When we returned to his place, he said I would be dropped off where he found me and that I had to leave everything he had given to me there. True to his word, he dropped me off in the park where he found me and relief just consumed me. I didn't have to have sex with anyone. Whew, my guardian angels must have been looking out for me.

After being left in the park, I contemplated my next move. Since I could not come up with a solution to the problem of having a place to live, I did the only thing possible: returned to the hell house. To my relief, I did not have to remain there because it had been decided I would be placed in a home for juvenile delinquents. I looked forward to going to the home. I was glad to be away from Lucy's hell house and Calee's house of torment.

The home was located within the city limits of Washington, D.C. It had several floors and very tiny windows, and was designed for kids like me who had committed minor offenses, such as running away from home. While there, I began to feel alive, like a real person who, for the first time in my life, didn't feel like the butt end of a joke, nor was I beaten or belittled. The home was my first experience with compassionate kindness.

One evening, a counselor called me aside and gently informed me my grandmother had passed. Not knowing much about my grandmother, I did not get upset about her passing. But the way the counselor talked to me elicited tears. Not because my grandmother had died, but because of the way this stranger delivered the message. I was not used to someone talking to me in such a soothing and compassionate way. I realized from this conversation that people could be kind, and I was shown a different way to interact with others. I have never forgotten the counselor's kindness and compassion.

My stint in the home, for the most part, was pretty uneventful. Yet during that time, I felt a freedom I had never experienced before. No one was on my back about doing things, nobody cussed at me, or tried to make me feel bad or miserable. I began to feel like I mattered, and my self-esteem grew a little. I learned new crafts and participated in fun activities, such as duck pin bowling. I also met my first boyfriend there. He was my first experience with interracial dating, and although we were not able to do more than talk to each other, I enjoyed knowing him. I did not know my stay at the home had a time limit until one day a counselor told me if I didn't return home soon I would be placed in a youth detention center. I did not fully comprehend what this meant until I was put on a bus heading for the detention center with what little personal belongings I had.

The center was located in a country like setting and was divided into two sections. The minimum-security section housed minor juvenile offenders, and the maximum-security section housed juveniles who had committed serious crimes, such as murder, assault, rape, kidnapping, and carjacking. Due to the nature of my crime, a run-away deemed beyond control, I ended up in the minimum-security section. Sometimes cliques formed and picked out one person to torment. At first, I looked on in horror when a person was singled out to be bullied, but after a while, it became commonplace to witness such things, so I decided to try my hand at bullying someone younger than me. I must admit, at first, it gave me a sense of power, but after a couple of times, it became something to do when I was bored. Bullying did not go over too well in the cottage where I was housed. After being warned once, I was transferred to the high-risk section when I didn't heed the warning. I did not like my new environment so I kept to myself in order to avoid confrontations with fellow residents. Most of them were far more hardened than I, and their conversations confused me. After being at the center for a year, I became obsessed with being free from the regimented life in which I was a participant of. I asked to be returned to my former residence, Calee's house, and the request was granted. I hoped we could peacefully co-exist, since I had been away from her for quite some time.

MARRIAGE AIN'T THE WAY

Before leaving the center, I was placed under the purview of social services. I reported to a counselor and received a clothing allowance. I do not know if Calee was given a stipend for me. I just know she was a little kinder and no longer complained about money.

After my return from the center, I helped around the house while pondering my future. I thought about college, and realizing I hadn't finished high school nixed that idea. I didn't know what to do with myself. Calee suggested I look for a man to settle down with, and if he was from the South, he would be a good catch. She tried hooking me up with someone she considered an eligible catch, but I could not connect with him on an emotional level.

I stayed around the house and did not go out because I feared being at the bad end of Calee's tongue-lashing. One night, she invited me to go to a party with her. It was my first grown-up affair and I was pretty excited about being treated like an adult. I felt as though I was finally being accepted as a person, so I happily accompanied her to the party where I met my future husband, that night.

The party was in full swing when we arrived and I felt out of place as I looked around the room in search of someone to talk with. Suddenly, this guy came over, introduced himself as Sylvester, and asked me to dance. He was a little darker than me, two inches taller, medium build, and said all the right things that made me feel special. We danced, and were inseparable for the rest of the evening.

From the start, our relationship was hot and heavily based on sex. I did not look into the type of person he was other than Calee seemingly approved of him. I don't remember how soon we started having sex, but it was very quickly after we met. Sex with him was always like a rocket hurtling through space toward the moon. In other words, he had the right size equipment and knew how to use it. He was a postal employee, which was considered to be a good source of employment at that time, was originally from the South, and he rocked my world in bed. After dating a short time, I got pregnant with my first child.

After the birth of my first child, I felt changed, different. Looking at the little person I brought into the world filled me with pride and hope for the future. During my three-day stay in the hospital, I had time to evaluate my life. My new focus became this little being who depended on me to love and take care of him, so I felt I needed to make new choices. I decided to return to Calee's house because I was a mother now and unsure if I wanted to stay with the father of this child. Besides, I had nowhere else to go.

When I returned to Calee's home, I figured I was a grown-up and that her spiteful, hurtful words were in the past. For a little while, she was pretty decent, providing advice in a kindly way and she seemed to enjoy my son. However, her kindliness was short-lived, and then a new set of "don'ts" were issued. Some of them were pretty ludicrous and amused me, such as "you can't go near the kitchen because you just had a baby and you are nasty", and "you can't go up and down stairs because it will pull your uterus down".

Because I insisted, Sylvester and I married when our son was a month old. The torrential downpour on our wedding day should have warned me that marrying him was a bad idea, but nothing at that time would have changed my mind because Calee seemed to lecture me about everything. My new husband and I stayed with her because we didn't have any place else to go for about two months after we were married. There were times when I felt she actually loved and cared about me, and then there were times when I felt like a frightened child again who was being forced to live by her standards, rules, and beat downs. My stay in her home consisted of her watching everything I did and complaining I wasn't doing things right. During the day, she bad-mouthed my husband, and when he came home, she bad-mouthed me. She seemed to dote on my baby though, and wanted to take care of his every need. There were times when I wondered why she couldn't care for me the way she cared for my baby. I decided not to dig into her dichotomy of treatment and just to go with the flow of the house so I could have some peace and not be belittled or bullied.

With nowhere else to go and still confused by Calee's actions, I tried to keep the peace by doing everything she asked me to do, and by staying out of her way as much as possible. I would get upset with her when she turned the heat off at night, saying she was saving on her gas bill because my husband was paying her rent. I was elated when she tenderly held my son and nicknamed him "Little Man". And when he was diagnosed with asthma, she provided nurse-type care until he felt better.

There was one incident when I felt Calee cared about me. My husband and I had a big verbal fight. He left and came back the next day, threatening to take our son to his mother to be raised. Calee implicitly told him, "take a child? You ain't taking no child out of here, you wait right here." She brought out her sawed-off shotgun and pointed it directly at him, saying, "If you touch that baby, you gone die today." He didn't say a word, just turned around and started running. We both enjoyed the moment. I because she was showing she cared how I felt, her because she was sticking up for something she believed was right.

After my husband and I made up and he returned to Calee's house, the daily put downs resumed. His bad habits were regaled during the day and mine at night when he came home. One day, I couldn't take it anymore and demanded he find us a place to live. He did, and when I informed Calee we were moving, a different put down began. She told me I wasn't going to treat my child right and that I wasn't going to be a good mother. I had no idea why she said those things to me and could only attribute her saying them as a way to hurt me and put me down yet again. I rallied my courage and refuted her diatribe by emphatically telling her that I was a good mother. I knew I was a good mother and her saying that I was going to be a bad mother to my child was the last straw for me. I'd had enough, and made up my mind I would never put myself in a position to be under her domination or roof ever again. I was doggedly determined to make a go of my marriage and to prove her wrong. Old resentments of the anger and fear I'd felt towards Calee and her spiteful words spurred me on to make the best of my life. Whenever I encountered difficulties in my marriage, and as a single parent, I would remind myself to keep pushing forward and that I would rather live outdoors than in her house again.

I got married when I was seventeen, mainly because I wanted to be out of the clutches of Calee, and because I wanted a life of my own with someone I thought cared about me. I had always imagined building a life with someone, perhaps starting out struggling, but eventually working as a team to have/acquire the best life had to offer. In the beginning, I felt my marriage was stable. It didn't feel like we were struggling because my husband took care of us. He came home every night, doted on the baby, and paid plenty of attention to me. Even though he drank every day, I never saw him drunk. It wasn't until after we moved from Calee's house that I noticed a change in his behavior.

We moved to a rooming house where we had two rooms on the top floor and shared a bathroom and kitchen with two other families. After living there a short time, I began to notice the owner of the house, who was female, and my husband drank every day together and I became concerned they were having an affair. After expressing my concerns, my husband assured me I was wrong and that they were just drinking buddies. I decided to keep a watchful eye on the two of them but could find nothing wrong with their sitting together, so I stopped worrying. But I remained watchful.

In the beginning, I knew my husband drank, but I did not know he was an alcoholic. I had no real concept of what living with an alcoholic was like until I married him and discovered alcoholism meant drinking every day, starting with breakfast, and that when in an alcoholic state, oppressive bullying is common. Sure, I had seen two cousins in inebriated states who drank every day and were called "wine-os", but hadn't lived with them on a daily basis, and it never entered my consciousness that I would end up living and suffering the repercussions of being in a house with that type of personality.

One evening, my husband and I had a big fight and I sent him to the hospital with a painful penis. We had been arguing and all of a sudden, he slapped me. Without a second's thought, I grabbed his penis and would not let go until I was sure he would not hit me again. He returned home from the hospital a quieter person and did not pick a fight with me for quite some time afterwards. When I became pregnant with my second child, I felt we needed to move to a bigger place where I didn't have to share a bathroom or kitchen with anyone else. So after much prompting on my part, we got a one-bedroom apartment. Once we moved into the apartment, I noticed real cracks in the marriage. My once adoring husband had several bad habits. He drank every day and began staying out all night, saying he got drunk and fell asleep. I tried every trick I could think of to get things back on track, including tears, anger, and hostility. I badgered him for a reason for the shift in his attitude towards me and for his everyday drinking. Often, the result of my inquisition would be hand-to-hand combat fights. Although normally I would rather run than fight, with him, it was just the opposite. He would slap me and I would hit him back, he would hit me again and I would hit him back, and so it would go until he gave up and went out of the door.

Sometime between our first and second child, he lost his job with the post office for cussing out the supervisor. According to him, the supervisor was disrespecting his manhood. I was not pleased. In fact, I was a little fearful of living without an income, but still, at that time I believed in him. He was able to find work as a truck driver for a local poultry company rather quickly. After a short while, we were able to move into a two-bedroom apartment, and my hope for a better future reared its head once again.

Even though my husband continued to drink every day, he took care of his family responsibilities. Often times when he got really drunk, our fisticuff problems would ensue. For no apparent reason, he would pick a fight and out of the blue, slap me. My response would be to hit him back and on several occasions, I sent him to the hospital because I would grab his penis either with my teeth or hands and would not let go until I felt confident he would not hit me again.

So went my life until after the birth of my youngest son. One day I was having one of those I don't feel ill, yet I don't feel well, kind of days so I was lying on the sofa when he came home. He asked for dinner and I told him I wasn't feeling well and that I wasn't fixing dinner, which set him off. He slapped me. This shocked me and while coming to terms with the fact that I had just been hit for no apparent reason, my youngest started crying. So I picked him up to comfort him and my husband slapped me again. After putting the baby down, I hit him back. The fight was on, with him hitting me and me hitting him back. However, the fight got to be a little too much for me and I went out of the bathroom window and called the police who came and reminded him he could not hit me. They forbade him from returning to the residence temporarily and told him if they came back, he was going to be locked up. That seemed to do the trick. When he returned home the next day, his whole demeanor had changed from menacing to kindly. As for me, I was incensed he started an argument and fought with me when I was not feeling well. I was incensed he hit me while I was holding the baby and broke my much-needed forty-eight dollar eyeglasses. I also felt humiliated that I had to flee from my home out of the bathroom window. A rage I had not experienced since childhood began to build inside me. The more I thought about what had happened, the less clear my thinking became, and when I looked at him, he no longer had human form. All I saw was a red blob-like substance that needed to be eradicated. I went into the kitchen and grabbed the biggest knife I could find, walked to where he was sitting, and told him if he ever touched me again, I was going to kill him. I said, "don't even look at me or I will kill you." I think he realized I meant business, and for the next two to three weeks, I slept holding the knife, hoping he would give me a reason to plunge it into his body. After the third week, my anger subsided and I began to notice whenever I changed positions in bed, his body would tense up or he would sit up as if he might need to run or defend himself. It amused me to know I could create fear in him, and sometimes I would turn or move deliberately just to feel his body tense up. I felt as though I had exacted revenge on him by making him afraid of me and I was ecstatic.

Things between us were wonderful again before they soured to the point of no return. Hubby was gainfully employed and we were getting along well. I felt that we were making progress and a new car was in order, so I went to work and saved enough to get a used vehicle. I thought our life together was moving forward and I loved the idea that we could improve our standing in life so *hope sprang eternal* within me again. I felt overjoyed about owning our first car, until I wasn't picked up after work one night.

After ending my shift around 10 p.m. one night, my boss offered to take me where I could easily hail a cab since it was late and my husband hadn't come to pick me up. About a block from where I worked, I spotted my car and asked my boss to pull over and let me out because I could get a ride home with my hubby. As I walked towards the car, I noticed the windows were steamy and that there were two people sitting extremely close in the car, so I walked up to the driver's side and looked in. There sat my husband and a former neighbor, kissing and embracing. I could not believe my eyes. I just stood there, staring first at him, then at her. All kinds of emotions came and went within me as I stood dumbfounded, looking into the window of the car at the two people entwined in each other's arms in a mean lip lock. After a brief moment, I walked away, deciding that the two of them could have each other.

Things were never the same between hubby and me after that. I knew I was going to get even with Sylvester for betraying my trust and for all of the heartache he had caused me in the marriage. Seeing my husband with another woman took a toll on my self-esteem and left me with a desire to feel wanted, desired, and whole again, so I decided to date my boss. The affair went on for quite some time and one night, when my lover dropped me off near the house, Sylvester spotted me getting out of his car. Of course, an argument ensued. Sylvester accused me of sleeping around and I denied his accusation. I didn't care what he thought or felt, I just did not want to get into another altercation with him, so I lied and said it wasn't me. I was not able to convince him that he was wrong and he was not able to convince me to change my story, so we settled into an uncomfortable co-existence.

FROM BAD TO WORSE

At some point, Sylvester lost his truck-driving job because he was caught stealing the company's merchandise. Money became scarce and he could only find ad hoc work helping other drivers make deliveries. Things became so bad I had to ask my lover to provide groceries for my children. As I cooked dinner from the food I was given, my anger towards Sylvester hit an all-time high and revenge thoughts set in. I finally decided I didn't want a physical fight, yet I wanted him to feel embarrassed and ashamed that he was not supporting his family. For the first time in a long time, and to my surprise, he came home sober. He saw the pot of food on the stove and grabbed a plate, but before he could sit down and enjoy one morsel of food, I told him my family had eaten and that he had better not eat what was left because I had spit in it. Looking at my face, I guess he believed me because he put the food from his plate back into the pot without touching it. Even though I had not spit in the food, it was the only thing I could think of to prevent him from eating what I had to ask another man to provide. Since he was afraid to eat, I felt smugly vindicated; justice had been served.

A couple of weeks later, I got a call from Sylvester saying he had been arrested. According to him, he had been caught stealing and would be in jail for a while. I was very angry, frustrated, and on the verge of despair until I looked in the faces of my children and realized I had to pull myself together. So off to the welfare office I went for temporary support. I received immediate food stamps, got a check, and was able to pay rent. There was a little left over for miscellaneous necessary things such as shoes and clothes for the children. Once Sylvester was out of sight, I began to realize how miserable my marriage had become yet, I couldn't figure out how to disengage from it. Upon his release from jail, Sylvester begged me to let him move back in. Although I knew if the welfare office caught him in the house, my assistance would be cut off, I relented and allowed him to move in. Jail seemed to have taken the sting out of his nature because he was no longer abusive and he diligently looked for work. Finally, he found steady work as a truck driver helper and I was able to cancel my welfare assistance.

The new Sylvester did not last long. He started drinking to the point of drunkenness again, staying out all night, and being verbally abusive. One day, out of the blue, he began punching our eight-year old son. He punched him so hard his nose started bleeding, all the while prodding him to be a man. The sight of blood coming from my child's nose infuriated me and a calm came over me that I had not experienced in quite some time. I stared at the scene before me for a few seconds and then readied myself for the fight to end all fights. Stepping between the two of them, I told Sylvester he'd better not hit my child again or we were going to war. He looked at me and, after a moment's hesitation, stopped his assault. I guess my face said it all. By this time, I was so furious with him and downtrodden about my marital situation, that I decided I wanted a divorce. I felt the marriage had outlived its usefulness and I could do better raising my children alone.

I considered Sylvester to be a nasty and verbally abusive drunk. After years of battles, I had grown extremely tired of the verbal and physical battles we constantly had so I began to pray for relief from my situation. Within a month, he fell and broke his ankle. He called from his hospital bed, asking me to come see him. The phone call infuriated me. My mind was ablaze with vivid imagery of all the hurts I had suffered during our marriage. I thought about the time he punched my son and caused his nose to bleed. I thought about the numerous times he came through the door, reeking of alcohol without bringing a penny into the household for food or shelter. I thought about the time he went to jail for six months leaving me with no money and three children to take care of. I thought about the physical fights we had when he demanded I go to work and take care of him and my children. The more I thought about the life I shared with him, the more enraged I became, so I borrowed money from a neighbor and went to the hospital.

Seeing him lying in the hospital bed fueled my rage. I verbally unleashed upon him all of the fury, anger, and frustration that had been building within me throughout the marriage. My first question to him was "how on earth was I supposed to get money to come see you when you hadn't given me any?" From there, I tore into him with a vengeance about all the wrongs he had done to me and, for the first time in my life, I cursed like a sailor. I told Sylvester he was no longer welcome in my home and I refused his requests to pick him up from the hospital. A friend of his picked him up and pleaded with me to let him return home because he didn't have any place else to go. I finally relented and let him back into the house with a warning that things had to change for the better or else we were through. Of course, things didn't get better. Even though I desperately wanted to be rid of Sylvester, I couldn't leave the residence because I didn't have any place else for my children and I to go. So every day I reminded myself that my marriage was over and he was going to be the one leaving.

My wish came true one cold January morning. Sylvester packed a bag and said he was leaving. I was thrilled to hear this; my wish was becoming a reality. On his way out, I reminded him he would not be permitted to return. Seeing him walk out the door was a joyous relief to me. No more stinking smelly feet, no more arguments with someone I despised, no more putting up with a bad attitude from someone I felt did not deserve to be near me, and no more of a drunken, disgusting, non-supportive, do nothing slob hanging around my neck.

To my surprise, two days after Sylvester left, the landlord came to set my children and me out on the street. I was horrified and afraid, but luckily, due to a friend's prompting, I had gone to the welfare office the day he left and applied for welfare. The welfare office paid the rent so we didn't get set out. They also gave me emergency food stamps. I was relieved and hopeful again, that is until Sylvester showed up at the door asking to see the children. I let him in with a reminder that he could not stay, that after he spoke with the children, he had to leave because this was my house now, not his. As soon as he came through the door, he informed me he was moving back in. Not heeding my response of, "oh no you aren't," he tried forcing his way to the bedroom and so another physical fight began. With fierce determination, I fought for the right to be left alone by him, for the right to raise my children in a better environment, for the right to have peace of mind, and for the right to be free from his tyranny. Finally, when he saw he couldn't force his way back in, he gave up and left.

ENOUGH IS ENOUGH

After the breakup of my marriage, an incident occurred which helped to solidify my resolve to be completely free of the marital phase of my life. When Sylvester walked out of the marriage, he handed me the keys to the car. After getting temporary help from the welfare office, I found work at a thrift store five minutes from my home. Upon getting off from work one day, I noticed my daughter, who should have been home doing her homework, standing by the car with her father. Gathering my courage, I walked over to the car, told my daughter to get in, and asked Sylvester why he was there. He responded he was here to take the car. I told him he could not have it. As I got in and started up the car, he got into the passenger side. I repeatedly asked him to get out, and the more I had to ask him, the angrier I got. It wasn't enough that he had left us penniless and without a means of support, but now he wanted to take the only mode of transportation my children and I had.

I lost all sense of reason when he reached over and snatched the keys out of the ignition while the car was in motion. Not fully aware of the car swerving from side to side and only faintly hearing my daughter calling my name, I yanked off my wig, hiked up my skirt, and turned the wheel of the car toward the curb. Then I began burning Sylvester with the lit cigarette in my mouth as I frantically grabbed at the keys with one hand and hit him with the other. He finally stopped fighting with me, jumped out of the car as the car hit the curb, and threw the keys at me. Before continuing to drive home, I managed to calm myself down after making sure my terrified child was all right. That night, Sylvester called, threatening to put sugar in the tank of the car. Fed up with Sylvester and frightened that he would actually harm the car, I decided the car was an unnecessary worry so I got my former boss to take the car off my hands.

That was not the end, though; it was the beginning of nightly phone calls. I can still hear his voice saying, 'I'm coming to get you, and I'll be there in ten minutes." Then he would hang up. Those calls kept me on edge and worried, which I am sure was his intention. Because I lived in an apartment that could be easily accessed, I worried he would break in, catch me off guard, and do me bodily harm. So I kept a pot of water boiling all the time and slept very little.

After a month of threatening phone calls, I hatched a plan to finally get rid of Sylvester. Knowing he did not want to go back to jail, I decided to put a scratch on my arm and to talk to the district attorney. We were both called into the DA's office and I pleaded my case, saying he left the residence, leaving me penniless with three children so I had to go on welfare, and that when I wouldn't let him return to the residence after he showed up at my door, he attacked me. I showed the DA the scratch on my arm as proof and said that I had a witness. Of course, Sylvester denied hurting me, but the DA didn't believe him and told him so. The DA informed him he could see the scratch on my arm, pointed out that I had a witness, and if he bothered me again, he was going to be locked up for quite some time. After we left the DA's office, Sylvester came up to me saying, "you know you lying. I didn't hurt you. I am through with you, I am just through with you." As I walked away smiling like the cat that swallowed the canary, I retorted, "I have been through with you." I walked away from the DA's office that day with a renewed sense of purpose and feeling of elation from the winning of a victory over an enemy, because that is what he had become.

After returning from the DA's office, I looked at the faces of my three young and innocent little beings and pondered my next move. I felt I could take care of my children because I remembered passing the GED test on my first try, and if I was smart enough to get a diploma without struggling to learn the material, then I was smart enough to pave my way in life. I believed I could create a better life for myself and my children, so I decided to look for a way to advance in life. I enrolled in a government-sponsored program for welfare mothers such as myself to learn typing and stenographic skills. It was a six-month program and paid a weekly stipend of seven dollars and fifty cents. I passed the class and took the federal government's typing and steno test and passed that with very high scores as well. I was hired immediately as a GS-3 clerk stenographer by the same program I had just completed. Now I could see my life beginning to progress. I was happy and my children seemed to be adjusting quite well.

While attending school, I approached an attorney I had met a while back and asked him to represent me in my divorce. He agreed and said the cost would be three hundred and fifty dollars, so I came up with the idea to use the money I received each week to go to school to pay down the cost of my divorce. There were two glitches. The first was that I had to pay one hundred and fifty dollars for Sylvester's attorney representation because according to District of Columbia law, a spouse must be represented whether he be physically present or not, which meant the party requesting the divorce is the one who pays for the other spouse's attorney. This news rubbed me the wrong way, but I had to keep reminding myself that my main objective was to get rid of Sylvester and that if paying for his attorney was what I had to do, then it was worth it to be rid of him. The second glitch was I needed a witness to support my claim that there had been no contact or cohabitation with Sylvester for a year. The witness problem was solved when I met Babs, who was also divorcing her mate and was in the same predicament as me. So we agreed to be each other's witness, even though we had only known each other for a short time.

I was able to pay my attorney and his attorney within a year. The court granted me a divorce, and sole custody of my children along with child support (which I never received a dime of). I finally felt totally liberated from someone I had grown to despise. While it was not uppermost in my mind, the anger of taking care of three children without financial support from their father would rear its ugly head whenever finances became a little strained. However, I used my anger to fuel my desire to make a better life for myself and my offspring. What I learned from my occasional anger about child support is that anger can be used in a constructive way if it's used to propel you forward into a better life. What I mean is I used my anger to harden my will to keep pushing forward toward my goals by taking one baby step at a time.

What I learned from a bad marriage is that I am a strong person who not only could support myself, but also three additional people. But the biggest lesson I learned is that I had to make choices and that I had to live by whatever choices I made.

THE PRICE OF FRIENDSHIP

A common belief today is you need friends in order to be a well-rounded individual. As far as I am concerned, the jury is still out on that one. My forays into the friendship zone rarely turned out to be in my best interests. I have always considered myself a true friend to others, but seldom, if ever, received true and sustained friendship from another. For a long time, I tried desperately to believe that everyone wanted the same things I wanted from friendship: a decent, honest person who knows who you are and loves you anyway. What I learned is there's nothing wrong with having friends, but be careful of the people you choose as friends.

For me, a friend's achievements were like my achievements. Even though on some level I knew the people I had chosen to be my friends were not my true friends, I felt as though I needed them to be. I wanted to feel I had value, that I could mean something to another, that my presence was good enough to be enjoyed, even if the other person had achieved a higher standing in life than me. The end result of these friendships always left me feeling empty and hurt because of their disrespect, callousness, or blatant disregard for my feelings (several so-called "close friends" got married and did not invite me to their wedding—some friend, huh?).

DO AS I SAY OR WE ARE NOT FRIENDS

I learned a very valuable lesson about friendship from Babs, the woman I met while attending clerk stenographic classes. I watched Babs attend class each day with either a scowl on her face or a look of desolation. Since we had common interests, a good, solid friendship developed until she called one day to tell me she had gotten married. I was deeply hurt that she had not included me in her wedding. It felt like I had been uprooted from the safe and comfortable place of being important to someone else to suddenly finding myself in a place of confusion, doubt, and fear, questioning whether I was a worthwhile person.

I decided to lick my wounds and continue with the friendship, but I withdrew from the deep connection I had felt with her. I could not understand, no matter how hard I tried, why I was left out of such an important part of her life when we were supposedly good friends. Even though we continued to communicate as two confidants, I began to call her less and less until one afternoon, Babs showed up at my home unexpectedly. I could tell by her facial expression that she had something on her mind and when I asked her what was wrong, she said she was not going to talk to me any more unless I started calling her. At first, I thought she was joking, but once I realized she wasn't, I was dumbfounded. I could not understand, nor would she provide me an explanation, as to why she was making this demand on me. I asked her if the numerous times I had talked with her on the phone and visited with her meant nothing to our friendship. The only explanation I got from her was that she was not going to call me any more unless I visited or called her. Her ultimatum not only angered me, but also made me feel betrayed and confused. After a brief moment of silence, I simply said "okay" and bid her farewell. As I stared at Bab's retreating back, I realized this was not a test of friendship; this was the end of a relationship. I instinctively felt our friendship had gone as far as it could go and had no value unless Babs dictated how our relationship should exist. I felt if I gave her what she wanted, I would allow myself to become a victim to be used at her whim. Being used by another human being in this manner was not acceptable to me, and I was not about to allow it to happen.

The last thought I had about Babs while watching her drive away was, "you ain't all that. And if you can be that cavalier about our friendship, then I don't need you in my life in any form, shape, or fashion." Her visit, although it made me sad, confused, and angry, gave me new insight into myself. I realized I had the right to live as I chose, that a relationship without mutual respect is no relationship at all, and that sometimes you have to put boundaries in place for your own spiritual safekeeping. I do not have to let someone bend me to their will. I don't have to be a victim of another human being, nor should I allow it to happen. I began to understand I could choose to leave toxic relationships or those that

57

lost their value. I can choose to stand up for my right to exist as an individual. I can value and honor me. Good lessons, don't you agree?

I have learned if you allow yourself to stress about the break-up of a relationship and continue reliving those memories and then obsess about what could have happened, should have happened, or would have happened in order to make the relationship work, you are a self-victim.

A self-victim is someone who continuously focuses on all aspects of what is no longer attainably available. A self-victim will walk around feeling sad, miserable, and depressed because what they want does not want them or is beyond their grasp. A self-victim will talk incessantly about what was lost to them, a car, job, marriage, girl or guy friend and unloving children, to anyone who will listen. A self-victim feels they have lost their self-worth because they are no longer desired.

Sometimes when someone you care about has victimized you, you feel as though that person ran you over with a vehicle. At least the pain can seem that great, especially when you realize you have given everything to them and they betrayed you or used you to the point where there is nothing left of you to use. It can seem like a long road back to the real you, and it is fraught with much self-doubt, pain, and self-discovery. But if you can picture in your mind's eye the end results you want to achieve and steadfastly hold onto that image, you will no longer be a victim of anyone, including yourself. I have found when you focus on a positive goal such as envisioning where you want to be, you heal more quickly because your mind is focused on something other than feelings of insecurity, chagrin, and angst. Those feelings can make you feel like you are slipping into madness.

Welcome to reality; where hell is revealed; and the
true identities of others; are forever concealed;
where god is everywhere; and so is the devil; and
you never know; if people are at your level, by
Masked Emotions

A SMILING FACE MAY SHOW NO TRACE OF THE REAL PERSON

My worst betrayal came by way of Abbey. Abbey and I met as we were entering our homes. From the start, we found a commonality in our lives, crappy husbands, illicit love affairs, and the pros and cons of motherhood. Our conversations became a therapeutic outlet for me and I soon developed a real fondness for Abbey and felt she was a good friend and confidant. I really loved having someone to share my feelings with and in turn, someone who shared their feelings with me. I don't know why our friendship changed from being good friends to one of enmity, but I noticed the change when my husband went to jail.

After Sylvester was incarcerated, I received financial support from a boyfriend. My youngest needed corrective shoes, which cost twenty-five dollars, so I asked for and received the money from my boyfriend. I shared with Abbey how grateful I was. Around the same time, Sylvester secretly returned to the residence and shortly thereafter, I got a call to report to the welfare office. I was not told why I had to report, just that I needed to come into the office for a conference. I knew if the welfare office found out Sylvester had returned, my assistance would be cut off immediately, and if I ever needed assistance again, I would have to jump through many hoops to get it, so I was very anxious about the conference. I met with my case manager and his supervisor the next day and was informed someone reported that Sylvester had returned to the residence and that I was buying my children twenty-five dollar shoes. I vehemently denied the allegations and to my relief, my case manager stuck up for me by telling his supervisor that he made a house visit and had found no indications that a man was living with me. Knowing I had only shared information about my life with two people, Calee and

Abbey, I approached the two of them and informed them about my inquisition at the welfare office. Both denied they had called and reported me. I believed Calee because knowing her personality, I figured if she had committed this act of betrayal, she would have said so. Even though Abbey denied any involvement, my gut told me it was her.

My next indication of her lack of friendship had to do with some missing pictures. After Sylvester and I separated for the final time, the affair with my lover heated up and he allowed me to take pictures of him in the nude. I don't recall what made me angry with my lover, but when it happened, my vindictive side took over and I shared with Abbey that I had taken compromising pictures of my lover. I didn't think any more about the conversation until the day I returned home from class and had an eerie feeling that someone besides my children and I had been in my home. Knowing how easy it was to get into the ground floor apartment, I cautiously walked through the rooms, looking for some sign of a break-in. I found nothing out of place, but the eerie feeling continued until I looked through my dresser drawers and discovered the compromising pictures of my lover were missing. Knowing that Abbey was the only one I had spoken to about the pictures and that that was the only thing missing, I began to put things together and realized my dear friend Abbey was not my friend after all. Instead, she was my Judas. Feeling crestfallen and betrayed, I had very little interaction with Abbey afterwards and shortly thereafter, I changed residences. I had no contact with Abbey once I moved until I ran into two of her daughters who pleaded for my phone number on behalf of their mother.

Abbey called and came for a visit. For a few moments, we sat in my living room in uncomfortable conversation. A couple of things about her struck me as odd. One of the things was her insistence on seeing my home. Since I was feeling uncomfortable with the way she asked, I refused. The other odd thing was the way she was continuously rubbing the coffee table, almost as if she was trying to replace the finish on it. I decided her actions were nutty and I wanted her to leave, but before I could tell her to go, she asked why I didn't come to her son's funeral. I had no idea her child had died, and I told her so. She insisted I did know and after denying her accusation a third time, I asked her how could I have known her son had died if she did not tell me. Her response was, "you knew, I know you knew." I stared at her incredulously, at a loss for words; and after a moment of my silence, she pasted a half smile on her face and left. That was the last time I saw Abbey, or ever want to see her again. No amount of pleading on her part would ever gain her access to my home again. I had had enough. The Abbey I had so dearly loved had turned into a lunatic.

My favorite relationship poem I wrote came to mind after Abbey's visit: **"What once there was, yet never was; and never meant to be has now become a thing of the past; so babe you're history."** Repeating this poem each time a thought appears about someone or something that no longer has value in my life not only helps me to focus on the present, but also gives me the strength and courage to keep moving forward away from could have, should have and would have thoughts.

I have never been one who requires or wants a lot of people to pal around with, and I live by the code of, "a friend is someone who knows who you are and loves you just the same." I now understand that not everyone can see the real you and/or like you. It doesn't make them a bad person just because they don't like you; it just means they were not the right person for you.

THE PROS AND CONS OF PARENTING

I must say that parenting was the hardest job of my life, but I knew that it had an expiration date, so I kept going. I always felt my role as a parent was to set a good example and instill good values. At times, it was difficult being a single parent, and I felt a little trapped, but when I looked at the faces of my children, I knew I had to make it work. Sometimes working two or three jobs in order to provide for my family left me exhausted and I wanted to run away from the everyday experiences of motherhood, but I kept going because I knew that I had to make it work.

My main parental goal was to train my children to fend for themselves, no matter what challenges they faced. I wanted them to have enough self-guidance to be able to thrive as an adult because I was not going to be around to pick up the pieces of their lives. I wanted them to understand if you want something, you need to work for it. I did not try to be their buddy, but I worked awfully hard at being the best parent I could be.

I never expected my children to be geniuses. I don't know what I would have done if they were. I knew they had good minds and I believed that whatever field of work they chose, they would do well in. When my children were growing up, a high school diploma was sufficient to reasonably take care of one's self, so I used to tell my children "eighteen is my limit, so you need to be making plans as to what you will be doing with your life." This was my way of trying to get them to understand they needed to make a choice about their life and that it had to be a choice that would assist them in surviving in the world, because living with mother as an adult was not an option for them--I had too many memories of how Calee's sister's children treated their parents.

When my two older children were growing up, they always had boisterous interchanges between them. My oldest son took pride and a certain pleasure in taunting his sister and she took pleasure in snitching on him and finding ways to get even with him for taunting her. Their verbal fights brought back childhood memories of the fights between Calee and her husband, so my initial reaction to their squabbling was one of fear. Once I remembered that siblings fought and that it was a way of working out their issues, I tried to remain neutral and not get involved. This usually didn't last very long because Annie, followed closely behind by her brother, would inevitably find me, trying to explain her side of the story. Meanwhile, her brother tried interrupting her with his version.

Staring at the two of them jockeying for a win in their latest battle would make me first turn inward and cringe as I did as a child. Their fighting brought back memories of the fights between Calee and her husband causing me to feel anxious, with a nervousness that I dared not show the two verbal combatants for fear that a show of weakness would lessen my authority. Most of the time, I just wanted to become invisible so I didn't have to play referee or listen to the latest episode of who's right and who's wrong. There were times when I wanted to beat some sense into them as a reminder to love each other and not to fight with one another. Once I pulled myself together, I halfheartedly listened to their plight, not caring who was right or wrong. I just wanted the fighting to stop and admonished them to quit fighting or they would both be punished for offending me with their story, attitude, and fighting. After the fighting stopped and the household settled down again, I would shake my head and wish I were somewhere else. I had to remind myself that the magical age of eighteen was coming.

From time to time, I called a family meeting because I knew people, places, and things could create temptation for my little ones. During these meetings, I reminded them they could be anything they wanted to be, that going to jail was inexcusable because jail was a choice, not an option. I'd remind them if there was something they wanted, they needed to work for it, "after all, I work every day," I would say. I'd also remind them that drugs were taboo. I did not take drugs and I would not tolerate them in my home. I wanted my children to be fully aware of what their boundaries were so the meetings helped me to define them.

When my children were young, I felt safe leaving them for short periods of time because as a single working parent, I had no choice. There wasn't money for babysitting, so a verbal warning of, "don't open the door for anyone," worked well. Having a tattletale in the house, my daughter, also worked well. I felt pretty confident some horrible incident would not occur while I was temporarily away because of my daughter's propensity for reporting on the behaviors of her siblings and for the telephone calls I made home while away.

Just because you are a parent does not mean you no longer have a need to be desired or feel wanted by someone other than the little bundles of joy you brought into the world. I made the choice not to feel guilty about leaving my children for brief periods. A brief period means a date once or twice a week, and usually home by midnight. Dating boosted my ego while providing a reprieve from parenthood. Sometimes it felt like a tonic that added just the right boost to my spirit whenever it needed lifting. I found when my spirits were lifted, I was a much happier person and enjoyed being a parent because I was able to give more of myself. I always understood that parenting did not mean turning off or shutting down an essential need and I knew I had to find a way to get mine met. I believe my dating philosophy turned out to be the right one because my children were pretty respectful to me with their dates, even though their dating choices and a few of their friends were not always to my liking.

I worried about my sons growing up without having a male figure to teach them things I knew I couldn't, so I prayed and asked God to send a guy that would teach the boys about manhood from a male perspective.

My prayers were answered when Russell came along. Russell was fun and attentive with the children, especially the boys, which was an answer to my prayers. Russell was thirty plus years my senior and four inches shorter than me, medium build, and possessed a great sense of humor. He took to the kids and the kids took to him. Right away. I was so relieved. I thanked God for sending Russell because he helped me fix broken things around the house, kept us all amused with funny stories and antics, wrestled with the boys, cooked for us, and generally became a family member. Lots of times, Russell saved the house from becoming a battleground by a funny antic or story, and I have always been grateful for him being part of our lives. Thanks to Russell, I stopped worrying about the boys becoming men and refocused my energy on providing for my family. Russell, my children, and I shared many good memories and he remained a part of our lives until his death.

Caring about your children does not mean you have to become a sacrificial lamb to be used in time of need and then abandoned. I learned if you allow your children to use your kindness and concern for them as a crutch you would be taken advantage of by them. Offspring can turn out far worse, than what you intended them to be.

How do you instill in your children the surety that you will help them, but not shoulder their burdens? I can't say one way is more beneficial than another. What I can say is when children reach a mature age, their lives are their own. Whatever mistakes they make must be shouldered by them. As parents, we can support them with empathy and sympathy and, if absolutely necessary, some financial support, but we should not be expected to continue being their sole support either financially or mentally when they are perfectly capable of supporting themselves. When we allow ourselves to become a post for them to constantly lean on, we have done nothing to help our children be the people they were meant to be.

"A mother is not a person to lean on, but a person to make leaning unnecessary." Dorothy Fisher

SACRIFICING WHO WE ARE IN FAVOR OF ANOTHER

I believe it is a mistake to sacrifice a basic need for the sake of our children. I've talked with numerous parents who have uttered the words, "If my child needs a pair of shoes and I need a pair of shoes, I will give my child a pair of shoes and go without shoes for myself." This statement never made sense to me. To me, if you don't have a pair of shoes, how can you sufficiently take care of your child? If you are shoeless, how are you able to work in order to support your child? I always found if my child and I needed shoes at the same time and I had very little money, we would both get shoes even if it meant getting them from a second hand store. While it is true parents will, and do, sacrifice for their children, a parent cannot or must not sacrifice what is basically needed to maintain one's self.

Sacrificing a basic human need eventually affects our mental state. Our attention is drawn away from our most fundamental responsibility of loving our offspring, to the fundamental need for survival. We lose our way sometimes when we go overboard with giving to our children. When we give until we deplete who we are, we have given too much and become our children's patsy or victim. So I ask you, where is it written that we have to be the victim of our children? Nowhere that I can find. Our only obligation is to provide for our offspring until they reach adulthood and then allow them to go on about their lives. As parents, we often say it's too hard out in society for my child to survive on his/her own. When we feel this way, we dwarf our child's ability to grow into a strong individual, able to meet life's challenges head on. Let's look at this another way. If you become incapacitated or you expire and your child has no recourse other than to fend for himself, what is your child going to do? Will he cave into the temptation of drugs or alcohol, thus rendering him helpless? Or will he step up to the plate, pick up the pieces of his life, and take on the responsibility of himself? If you taught your child through word and deed that it is okay to depend on someone else for survival, and that it is okay to shirk responsibility for himself, you created a person who feels hopeless, lost, aimless, and angry at the world. This individual will feel the world owes him something just because he exists in the world and will use whatever means of guile he/she can get away with to get needs met. An adult will show an inclination for this type of irresponsibility when they blatantly lie to you, then beg and plead for your forgiveness while continuing to do whatever made you unhappy in the first place.

When you have been hurtfully lied to by your children, a hole is created inside of you that never seems to completely disappear. It is very hard, if you ever can, to completely trust the person who violated your trust in some manner. So what do you do? Once your child has reached adulthood, you start by not accepting the blame for their actions. You did not do the deed, your child did. Please let these words sink in. Your offspring is responsible for any wrongful acts he/she committed, not you.

Before children reach adulthood, we need to shelter them from anything that may cause them harm. Once they reach adulthood, we may wind up sheltering ourselves from dealing with their situations. Sometimes being a parent means reaching an impasse in our thinking. We wonder how we got to be in the desolate and lonely place we find ourselves. We feel stagnated, stressed, and victimized by the callousness of our loved ones. We may even feel powerless to change our experiences with them. We shelter our psyche by rationalizing disrespectful behavior and maltreatment. Sheltering our psyche can take many forms. We may swallow our pride or allow pride to take the place of common sense when we have been insulted. We may erupt in angry outbursts and shout out retorts when we have been hurt, give ultimatums we know are impossible to keep, or allow ourselves to be victimized in some way. We may even allow bad tempered interchanges to continue because we see no other way to have a relationship. Sometimes we complain broken-heartedly to a confidant, yet say nothing to the offending person. We turn a blind eye to our loved one's antics, because we believe the pain of what's happening is too much to bear. We may even turn to sex, alcohol, food, or drugs for comfort.

Life has taught me that you can't control someone's loyalty. No matter how good you are to them, doesn't mean they'll treat you the same. No matter how much they mean to you, doesn't mean they'll value you the same. Sometimes the people you love the most, turn out to be the people you can trust the least. Trent Shelton

LETTING GO OF THE ADULT CHILD

What I have come to understand is that sometimes parent/child relations are not destined to be ongoing. I realize we have fulfilled our parental obligation when the individual carrying our genes reaches a point in their existence that our teachings are no longer of benefit to them. They no longer need us to tell them right from wrong. They no longer have to be in our good graces in order to survive in this world. They are dealing with, or habitually not dealing with, their own mistakes. Their expectations of and for themselves may be different from our expectations of them. At a certain point, if an adult fails to live by their own standards, values, and mores, they have done themselves an injustice. It is not our responsibility to automatically do without things that we need in order to constantly assist a grown up, even if we are the vehicle for their entry into the world.

I believe we are here, living on this earth, to learn how to love. But learning how to love is not always an easy task. Sometimes love means letting go of whatever needs to be released, no matter how painful it may seem at the time. Sometimes love means saying "no". This can be a tough one because as parents, we want to see our children happy. It may or may not be helpful when we say, "I don't want my child to go through what I went through". Life happens for everyone, whether we want it to or not. It is not our place to judge or try to stop the life experiences our adult offspring have to go through in order to learn lessons. Sometimes love means silence, because it is not helpful if we allow ourselves to become the "yes, can do" person at every bump in the road our adult child experiences. It's not helpful if we keep our adult children from experiencing learning about life by picking up the pieces each time they fall. We can be helpful if our children try everything possible to help themselves first. It is just not helpful or loving to have a child persistently cling to their parents for emotional or financial support.

In order to let go of the adult child, we must first realize that the child is no longer a child. The person who was once a child is now an adult who needs to make choices for him or herself. He/she is an adult human being who is now operating on his or her own mores and values. No matter how hard you may have worked to instill great values in your child, the bottom line is he/she will live according to what he/she deems appropriate for his/her existence.

Once you realize that everyone, and I do mean everyone, has to travel their own path individually, it becomes easier to cut the apron strings. I am not talking about the child who has medical needs and has to remain in their parent's care. I am talking about able-bodied adults who are perfectly capable of finding their own way in life. If you find it too difficult to let your adult child go all at once, take baby steps. Withdraw from doing things that the adult child should be doing for him or herself, such as laundry. Set up some new boundaries that allow you to feel more peaceful in your surroundings. Make up a list of things you want to experience for yourself. You can call it your bucket list. Start doing things that allow you to be happy and peaceful. Once you start living a life that's just right for you, you will find it much easier to let go and allow your adult child to live their own life.

LIVING WITH THE GOOD THE BAD AND THE UGLY

In the beginning stages of parenthood, I never dreamed it was possible that three individuals brought up in the same household under the same guidance would require such diverse parenting techniques. I also never took into consideration that three individuals under my roof would deploy their own tactics and understanding in such dissimilar ways in order to relate to their environment. I now know better.

Whenever I spoke with anyone about my children, I used the title of the movie, The Good, the Bad and the Ugly (*The Good, the Bad and the Ugly*. Dir. Sergio Leone. United Artist, 1966.) to describe them, because I found I was forced to use different methods to get their attention or cooperation. For instance, when going to the library. As a library patron, everyone is expected to sit quietly in the facility, and to be in compliance with library rules. With one child, I could say, "sit down and be quiet," and that child did exactly as asked. With another child, I needed to enforce my request with a warning-type look that said, "if you don't do what I am telling you to do, you and I are going to have an issue". That child would look at the expression on my face and then do exactly as asked. With the third child, not only would I have to say sit quietly and follow the request with a warning look, but I would also have to take him out of sight in order to let my hand have a conversation with his butt to get this one to cooperate. Different child, different method, even though they were all raised under the same roof.

LIVING WITH THE "GOOD"

Andy was, and still is, one of those individuals I describe as born with an old soul maturity. During my pregnancy with him, I always felt as if love flowed from him to me. He was an affectionate child and always had a ready hug for me. He usually stayed out of trouble, which gave me a respite from his older siblings. His loving nature was a blessing to me because it showed me there could be an alternate way to feel about a family member; and that it was important to show love. Sometimes his affectionate nature helped me be a little more understanding with the two older children. At age fourteen, though, he seemed to turn overnight into a replica of his older siblings, with a blatant disregard for household rules. He did nothing majorly wrong, nor was he disrespectful, but he began exhibiting a stubbornness to do things his way that I had not experienced from him before, and he was no longer affectionate. I was dumbfounded, and had no explanation for the change and did not know how to reach this new person. So I started withdrawing from interacting with him. Feeling hurt while fighting anger at the situation, and totally confused, my new wish became "Lord, let these individuals hurry up and get out of my sight". I held onto this wish until Andy reached sixteen. Then one day, he apologized to me for the way he had been acting, hugged me, and said he would do better. I didn't quite believe him, so I responded with "we'll see."

True to his word, he was obedient to house rules and did extra things to make me happy. Once the other two were out of the household, Annie in her own place and Junior on his gadabouts, I finally had the peaceful home I had always yearned for with a loving individual. It became a pleasure to come home in the evening and not a chore. Andy became what's called my running partner and nicknamed me "Chief". We went to a lot of places and did a lot of things together and our temperaments were similar. He turned into the kind of person that gave me bragging rights and I used to say, if I knew all my kids would be like Andy, I would have had a houseful of children.

I never had to ask him to cut the grass or do things around the house; when I got home, these things were done. I knew I could trust him, so he had carte blanch use of my car. He was the kind of kid that picked me up from work on time every day. I realized he had achieved a PhD in my reactions to life when he called me at work one day and told me that the car had a flat tire. Before I could say a word, he said "now I know what you are going to say, but." Each and every explanation he gave as to why a brand new tire was flat started with, "now I know what you are going to say." By the time he was through with his explanation, I was chuckling to myself and still do whenever I think about that particular conversation. He took on the responsibility of making sure the dealer replaced the tire. I was so proud of the way he handled the situation and was glad my faith had been restored in parent-child relationships. So my new saying about parenthood became, "one out of three ain't bad".

Things became strained again when he joined a religious sect and pretty much stopped communicating with me. I was heartbroken, but kept repeating to myself "my son loves me, I know he loves me," over and over. To my relief, he cut himself loose from the religious sect and started communicating with me again. Now I refer to him as the prodigal son. He's grown into a man I admire and respect, not only as a person to love, but also as a man within his own right.

LIVING WITH "THE BAD"

"Sometimes I'm mad and sometimes I am sad. I give it my all and I still feel bad." If this sounds like you, you are not alone. I spent years trying to figure out what I did wrong, why someone who passed through my body was so irritated, spiteful, and hostile to me, why she scorned me and/or would not speak to me, why someone I cared or tried to care about was so distant. I tell you, I cried so much that if there was a dry lakebed near me, I would have filled it up. And still I remained confused because I couldn't figure out how to fix the relationship.

I did not feel the warmth and closeness with my second child that I felt carrying my other two children. You know, the feeling that you're carrying a little human being to love. I felt as though I was a being used as a shelter to house a human being. When my daughter was born, even though I wanted a daughter, I did not feel the same tenderness I felt when my other two children were born. A part of me felt somewhat disconnected from the little, helpless person I had just given birth to while the other half of me felt concern for her wellbeing. Even though I felt protective towards her, there seemed to

73

be an impenetrable wall existing between us that did not come down until she became a toddler.

The funny thing about my daughter is that, years later, when she had a daughter of her own, she remarked she had the same feelings about her daughter and that she had only had a change of heart when a friend told her the child she had brought into the world may have to bring her a glass of water someday. Her revelation started me wondering if I had been carrying the burden of our relationship. I began to realize that it wasn't totally my responsibility, once she reached adulthood, to carry the brunt of the relationship. I did not have to accept whatever attitude she displayed toward me, and I certainly did not have to give her the power to make me feel bad about myself. I did not want to place all of the blame for our rift on her, but I learned from the treatment I received from her that I did not have to be a victim performing the function of a doormat either.

Annie was the middle child and always seemed to want more, and to have her own way. The first shock I experienced from Annie was when she stole my last five dollars. Before that, I considered her my little angel. She always seemed to do the right thing. At first, I didn't know which child took it, but after going to the elementary school where the two oldest attended, I found out through another child that Annie had five dollars taken away from her by some classmates. I was heartbroken, and just couldn't understand why she would take money from me. No matter how hard I tried after that incident, I was never able to shake the feeling that she wasn't completely honest with me, was doing something underhanded, or was just plain lying about something.

Annie, whom I fondly refer to as the house stenographer, always tattled on her two siblings. Her daily report about their misadventures used to get on my last nerve. She would start her report the minute I came through the door, sometimes before I could put down my purse. In retaliation, Junior would chime in with his report of the day. There were times when half of me just wanted to scream at the two of them "shut up, just shut up!" The other half of me would listen in order to know what was going on so I could rectify the situation. I felt trapped between wanting to know what was going on in my household and wanting a peaceful evening.

One May, I had to report for two weeks active duty at a time when Annie was graduating from the sixth grade. Not wanting her to miss her graduation, I asked Calee if she could stay with her while I was gone. Even though I felt there would be some conflict between the two of them, I hoped nothing major would occur. Bad thinking on my part. I should have just had her miss her graduation. While on tour, I checked in on Annie and there was a major hair battle going on. Calee was trying to comb Annie's hair and Annie was refusing. Being some distance away and not knowing what else to do, I told Annie to allow her hair to be combed and to obey the rules of the house. I thought they had worked things out, but to my chagrin when I returned to pick up my daughter, I got the longest report from Calee detailing Annie's faults and an angry Annie detailing Calee's faults. Due to the outpouring of emotions from the two of them, I felt horrible and as though I was caught between a rock and a hard place. In actuality, I did not care who was at fault. I just wanted them both to shut up. Trying to make peace between the two of them made me realize one thing: that was going to be the last time any of my children would stay with Calee for any reason.

Within a week of returning from my tour of duty, I got a call from Calee stating Annie was calling and harassing her on the phone, that she was trying to change her voice, but that she knew it was her. I apologized and told her I would take care of it. Annie denied making the phone calls, but something inside of me felt she was lying. So I told Annie if the phone calls continued, and if I found out she was lying, she was going to get a whipping. Needless to say, the phone calls stopped.

A SHIFT IN PERSONALITY

I noticed a big personality shift in Annie when she became a teenager. She went from talking to me to barely speaking to me at all. It seemed she was in her own world, but since she wasn't causing me any problems and I was going through turmoil with her brother, I didn't pay as much attention to her as perhaps I could have. Between her brother's antics and her walking around with a chip on her shoulder, I began to feel trapped again. There seemed to be no rest from what, at times, seemed like an intolerable situation. Some days, I would say to God, *Lord, I know we all get paid back for things we have done, but did you have to pay me back twice?"* But then I would remember everything has an expiration date and that put me back on track in my role as parent.

From the time my children could talk and understand what I was saying, I reminded them they would have to go to work at some point in their lives in order to take care of themselves. If they asked for something I could not afford, I used to sing them lines from a song by the Silhouettes called "Get a Job." They learned from experience that, when I sang that song, it was case closed, end of discussion. This song came in real handy with my daughter one summer. She kept asking me for a pair of Calvin Klein jeans. I tried explaining to her I didn't pay thirty-eight dollars for my pants, and asking her why she would want to pay to wear somebody else's name on her hind parts didn't work either. After saying "no" to her plea for the third time, I quit answering. I put a smile on my face and kept singing, "Get a job, sha na, sha nan a nan a, bu dum yip get a job, sha nan a nan a na." Case closed. She found a job and paid for her own jeans, to my relief.

At fourteen, Annie found a job working in a supermarket and started dating some guy I nicknamed the Jack Rabbit. When she brought him home and introduced him, he was skittish and seemed out of place. I couldn't get a handle on him, so I told Annie I didn't think he was the right guy for her and that she should be careful interacting with him. My instincts proved to be on target when I discovered marijuana in Annie's room.

In my home, there was an unspoken rule: leave your room messy and it affords me the opportunity to investigate. I used a messy room as an opportunity to find all of the hidden stuff the kids didn't want me to see. When Annie went off to work and left a messy room, I went through her shoeboxes and drawers and looked under her bed. When I looked under the mattress, I found a large bag of marijuana. After a few "OMGs", I focused on how to deal with the situation. So when Annie came home and went into her room, I followed her with the bag of marijuana. Holding up the bag, I asked why this was in my home. She replied it belonged to Jack Rabbit and said she was just holding it for him. I gave her a strong warning to never bring dope into my home again. Not satisfied with the warning I had given her, I wanted to know if she had succumbed to a pot habit, so I asked her why on earth would she hold an illegal substance for someone else and what was she thinking in doing so. Her answer was to silently shrug her shoulders. Not getting what I called a suitable answer to my questions and beginning to feel irate, I bade her follow me to the bathroom where I flushed the bag of marijuana down the toilet over her protests. I then told her to tell Jack Rabbit that he was not welcome in my home any longer, what I did with his marijuana, and if he had any questions about his dope, he should talk to me. Thank God I never found dope on my premises again. Annie was angry with me, but I did not care. Dope of any kind was a no-no. I did not do dope and I was not going to permit anyone living under the roof I paid for to have it in my home, either. I don't know what happened to the relationship between Jack Rabbit and Annie, but I never heard another word about him, nor did I see him again. I think Annie had to reimburse him for the dope because her funds seemed low for a while. I was not concerned about her financial situation because she was still a teenager living under my roof, which meant at least her basic needs were met.

After graduating high school, Annie got a job working for the housing authority. Hoping she had grown up enough for me to trust her, I added her name to my credit card. I cautioned her about overspending and told her she would need to pay for the charges she made, to which she agreed. When I got the credit card statement, I was flabbergasted that she had charged eight hundred dollars in one month. It wasn't that she had made such a large purchase, it was the timing of the purchase. She waited until I had gone to summer camp and never said a word about the large purchase when I returned. I took her name off of my account immediately and had her open her own account, transferring the eight hundred dollars to it. Now we were back to square one because I could not shake the feeling of being betrayed by my own flesh and blood whom I had trusted to do the right thing. Could have, should have, and would have ran rampant in my mind about my daughter and, at that time, I felt no need to change my way of thinking. I only knew I felt justified in feeling the way I did.

Late one night, I received a call from what sounded like an elderly desperate woman who identified herself as Annie's boyfriend's grandmother, asking me to please have my daughter stop harassing her. She said Annie was threatening to have her put out of her home because she was keeping her boyfriend from seeing her. This statement rang true for me because, at the time, Annie worked for the public housing office and since the caller lived in public housing, it seemed plausible to me. She also informed me Annie was taking cabs to her house, demanding to see her grandson. Not wanting to believe my child could be this heartless, yet knowing that by her very nature she could be vindictive, I confronted her about the telephone calls and the cab visits to the lady's house. She denied she had done any of the things I questioned her about. I wanted desperately to believe her, but something inside of me would not allow this to happen. So I told her I couldn't prove she was doing any of the things I was called about, but that it was wrong to threaten someone in that manner and that if she were guilty of doing any or all of these acts, she was to stop immediately. Apparently, my instinct was right, because I never received another call about my daughter harassing this elderly lady.

To my relief, when Annie had saved enough money, she moved into her own place. I was content to have her visit or call whenever she thought about it or whenever we were on speaking terms. In an effort to help her have a good start with her first apartment, I gave her permission to take whatever furniture she thought she could use. I thought when I told her she could have furniture, she would use common sense, but instead, I was reminded of how self-absorbed she was every time I looked at the empty living room. The two boys could not believe their eyes and complained bitterly that she had taken all the furniture, which left the house empty. I guess I didn't learn the lesson the credit card taught me, so I now added greed to my repertoire of Annie's negative character traits.

Annie met the love of her life at work. I dubbed him the uncomfortable hider because whenever I came around, he always seemed to be itching to be somewhere else or he would hide in another room. One day, Annie called to say she and her boyfriend had a fight, that he had drawn a knife on her, and asked me if she could stay with me. Knowing her temperament, I half believed the story she was telling me because it just felt like something was missing. However, she was my daughter and not wanting to see her hurt, I agreed that she could move in, but that she would have to contribute one hundred and ten dollars per month to the household. It wasn't about the money, I just did not want her to sponge off of me. In the beginning, things were nice and we got along fairly well. I don't know what changed, but suddenly she stopped talking to me and started closing her bedroom door. I became perplexed and perturbed at the change of attitude and I started to become annoyed with her. We were like two strangers passing each other with one going east and the other west. Thinking she was hiding something like drugs again, I searched her room when she wasn't there, but did not find anything. Not wanting to tolerate this type of situation, I asked her what was going on and if she was planning to move. Her response was an undiscernible answer and a shoulder shrug. Although frustrated, I didn't ask any more questions, but vigilantly waited for the next shoe to drop.

It didn't take long. One day at work, I got a call from an apartment manager inquiring how much rent Annie was paying. The phone call caught me off guard and I told the caller that she was contributing to the household, not paying rent. When I asked Annie why she did not tell me she was looking for a place so that I wasn't taken off guard, she answered she didn't think she had to. Her response annoyed me and deepened my distrust of her.

About a week later, upon arriving home, the house felt unusually quiet. Finding nothing out of place, I looked in Annie's room and discovered she had moved out and left her room in shambles. This was my breaking point. To my way of thinking, the way she moved out was sneaky and uncalled for and I was torn between feeling hurt and seething with anger. Once she left, I could not think about her without remembering the way that she left. I felt betrayed, and I could not understand why she did things the way she did.

After much soul searching, I could not find common ground upon which we could maintain a relationship. I thought about all the times I had trusted her and was left feeling betrayed. I knew I had reached a point where I'd had enough. I was in sink or swim mode and was no longer interested in putting myself in a position to trust her ever again. The emotional turmoil brought on by this incident caused me to make a decision to toughen up and not continue being a patsy or a victim to be used at the whim of Annie.

Two weeks after she left my home, she showed up at the door one night around 8:30 with bags in hand. Still angry with her, I stopped her at the door and, taking a tough stance because I'd had enough of her antics, and began to question her. I asked why she left the way she did, why had she left the room in shambles for me to clean up, and why had she left without even saying "goodbye" or "thank you". Then I asked where had she been for the last two weeks. She replied she just left because she had a place to stay, but now she was living in a shelter. I was too angry with her to allow her back into my home and so I did one of the hardest things I have ever done in my life. I told her that wherever she had been staying for the last two weeks was where she needed to go back to. I knew her circumstances would either make her or break her, and that she had to decide. I knew she was fully employed, headstrong, and driven to have her own way. And I also knew I was not helping her be an adult by having an open door for her to come and go as she pleased without having the full responsibility of taking care of herself. It was very difficult for me to watch her walk away with bags in hand, shoulders slumped, crying, but I stuck to my guns and did not waiver. Apparently, it was a turning point for her also, because soon afterward, she began her career as a law enforcement officer.

When Annie joined law enforcement, I was astonished and proud. I was astonished at the attitude shift on her part from being a victim in life to a participant of life. I felt she had finally come into her own as a young adult. I was proud she had achieved a goal and so I decided to let bygones be bygones, and that our past differences would be forgiven, at least on my part. When she, her brother, and I were together, we shared laughter and enjoyed each other's companionship. When she invited me to her graduation, I couldn't have been more pleased, so I carried a bouquet of flowers to present to her as I handed her the certificate of graduation she had earned. Sometime during the ceremony, she came over and told me she did not want me to present her certificate to her after all. When I asked why, all she would say is "I don't want you to, so please don't come up on stage." I hid my disappointment, hurt, and confusion by plastering a smile on my face as I gave her the flowers after the ceremony and congratulated her on accomplishing her goal. I did not understand what made her change her mind and she offered no explanation, so I buried my feelings inside me. But the chasm between us grew wider.

With the arrival of my second grandchild, her first, I had reached a stage in our relationship of acceptance and of wait and see. I accepted that she was who she was, that our relationship was probably about the best it was ever going to be, and I had adopted a wait and see how or if we could maintain a workable relationship. For a while, things were peaceful between us and I thought we were on good terms at last. After her second child was born, I noticed a reversion to the old Annie. I couldn't put my finger on it, I just felt like something was missing and there was a subtle anger just under the surface of her demeanor. Since there were now two little ones, I wanted to get to know them separately first, as individuals, and then spend time with them together, but there always seemed to be an excuse as to why they couldn't spend time with me and I was only permitted to be with the two of them occasionally. I finally gave up asking. It was then that I understood why some people just walk away from other people. The drama you have to go through in order to be a part of someone's life sometimes is just not worth the hassle. I decided that to try and force the issue of being with or seeing the grandchildren was more than I could go through. So I left them alone, except in my prayers, and I hoped for the best. Right or wrong, it is a decision that, to this day, I still stand by.

In an effort to establish a relationship with my oldest grandchild, I asked to spend some time with him. I made arrangements with his mother to pick him up from the airport, but Annie made different arrangements with his mother and picked him up instead. I was taken aback but decided not to make an issue of the change in plans. Figuring this might be a good time for Tony to get to know his cousins, I called Annie. We made an agreement that Tony would spend time with her during the week, but I would spend time with him on the weekend. When the weekend arrived, I called Annie to arrange a time to pick up Tony and was asked to take all three grandchildren. Since I had never spent alone time with Tony and he was only going to have a short visit, I told her that I wanted to get to know Tony since I had never spent time with him and that I would spend time with the other grandchildren later. I also asked her to explain to the other grandchildren that we would do something at a later date and that this time, it was Tony's turn to spend time with me. I had planned to do something special with them after Tony left. I got a call back from Annie saying that she had planned a picnic and that Tony would be attending that instead of visiting me for the weekend. I was furious. I took her action to be interference, downright manipulation of the situation, and a way of pitting her will against mine. I considered her maneuver a cheap shot on one hand,

and vindictive on the other, and geared to hurt me in some manner. I didn't argue with her because I did not want the drama, so I called Tony's father and explained the situation to him. Needless to say with that one phone call, Tony spent the weekend with me. After Tony left, I called to get visitation with the other two grandchildren and was told that my granddaughter couldn't come because she hurt her leg and that she did not want to separate them, so my grandson couldn't come either. Not knowing if this was another ploy by Annie, I decided to curtail visits with grandchildren and her. I did not feel like trying to force the visitation because I had reached a point of no return. I could no longer contain the anger I felt toward Annie. I was no longer able to think of her without feeling that she wanted to hurt me for some reason, which I could not understand. At that time, I was unable to reconcile the polar opposite of her vindictiveness towards me with my wanting to compassionately forgive her transgressions. I didn't want to feel the effects of her vindictiveness. I was not of a mindset to place myself in a position to feel her scorn again. Not wanting to cause a further rift, I settled for secondhand information about my grandchildren whenever Annie felt like talking.

I learned a very valuable lesson from this experience with Annie. The experience made me understand why some people walk away from people they love without going back. I no longer judged any man or woman from walking away from a situation without getting the whole story. Now when a man says I don't want the mama drama, I quite understand, because I don't want the daughter mama drama either. What I will always remember about the situation with my grandchildren is that I chose to live apart from them without asserting any grandparental rights. I chose to not feel guilty because I don't get to see them. I chose to pray for their well-being even though I do not see them. I chose to love them and to wish the very best for them. I realized that I could carry my love for them in my heart and feel blessed to do so. I could have chosen a different way of doing things, but I chose to be free from negative emotional drainage. I chose not to place my spirit in the position of having to feel imposed upon. I chose not to be bullied by my child. I chose to work on forgiving my child so that I could live in peace. Not for her sake, but for mine.

When Annie grew into womanhood, I thought we could establish a different relationship. I figured having her own children might make a difference in her personality, so I asked her to come to my house by herself one day. Sitting across from each other, I explained that the reason I wanted to see her was to apologize to her and I asked for her forgiveness for any wrong I might have done her. All I got was a nod and an "okay". Nothing changed, it made no dent, and I was no closer to having a viable relationship with her. Realizing I had done all I could with no seeming change, I began to let go and started putting less and less effort into making our relationship work.

The one thing I learned from the experience with my daughter is that you reach a point where you realize that, to continue feeling the deep hurt and pain associated with a person with no relief, is detrimental to you in every way. I reached such a point after I had cried a lake full of tears and was on the verge of deep depression. Perhaps my daughter feels justified in her treatment of me, I may never know. What I do know is that whatever wrong she thinks I have done to her will not and cannot compensate her in any way unless I give her the power to hurt me in some manner. And I won't be doing that.

CHANGE WILL COME

I had an epiphany the day I sat staring out my bedroom window at the cloud formations. I realized I could not continue to feel distressed about someone who appeared hell-bent on being vindictive towards me. I no longer felt I had to be a victim in our relationships. I came to realize that two people have to work on repairing a relationship together; one person cannot repair it by them self. I also realized since I had done everything humanly possible to have or maintain a relationship with my offspring and had gotten nowhere. I knew it was time to let go. Yes, that's right. I just let go of her. I let go of my need to have a daughter. I let go of my need to have or maintain a relationship with my daughter. I began to practice forgiveness. First, I practiced forgiving her for not being who I wanted her to be, and then I practiced forgiving myself for wanting her to be something she wasn't. Even though there were times when old, buried hurts that seemed unshakeable arose from somewhere deep inside, I kept at it, and the more I practiced forgiveness, the better I felt.

If you have forgiven yourself for any mistakes you made with your loved ones, it's time to let go. In the beginning, forgiving yourself can be difficult to achieve, especially if you have buried emotions that you are not consciously aware of. My advice is to start by realizing that forgiveness is the key to being free of emotional angst. Unless you forgive yourself and others, all pain you feel inside will persist and result in harming you physically in some manner, whether it be aches or pains, or living in perpetual sorrow. Once you come to the realization that you must forgive, start repeating over and over "I forgive (fill in the blank)". At first, it will seem strange, but after a while, you will begin to feel hope and then you will actually feel forgiveness towards the person, yourself included. If you have reached a point in your life where you realize that to continue down a path of reaching out to this person means the death of your essence, it's time to let go.

So the lessons I learned cover a lot of ground. I learned that I don't have to be a doormat for a loved one, no one can hurt me unless I give them permission to do so, and loving anyone does not mean we have to share the same space or values. I don't have to feel bad because of the actions of someone else, nor am I responsible for another's actions. I am a human being who loves, and in loving, I can let go of others for my sake or theirs and place their care and well-being in the hands of God.

A line from a Donnie McClurkin song has become my motto when I think of my daughter: "After you've done all you can, just stand." Even though Annie passed through my body and carries my genes, she either holds a grudge against me for some unknown reason or is just plain spiteful and deceitful. Either way, I am disinclined to be around someone, flesh and blood or not, who deliberately seeks to hurt me in some way. I have come to accept that our relationship served its purpose and now it's time to "Let go and let God."

LIVING WITH THE "UGLY"

I have come to understand that a mentally disturbed person lives in much the same way as a prisoner does in an institution. Incarcerated people live in a confined area (institution) in which their movements are curtailed and they are given clothing, three meals a day, and a bed. A mentally disturbed individual receives food, shelter, and clothing while participating in whatever fantasies he is experiencing in his mind at the moment (mental incarceration). The only difference is, when you are mentally incarcerated, you may be able to move about freely in time and space, whereas a prisoner of an institution cannot.

Living with a person who sees life in ways that seem desperate, full of folly, and out of this world is not an easy task. Not only do their insights and convictions make you question life itself at times, but also your take on reality. When you live with this type of person, your life feels as though you are trying to operate a bike with broken pedals. The pedals seem to have a mind of their own and no matter how much you try to get them to cooperate by placing them in the right position, your feet wind up on the ground. That's the way I feel about my oldest child. All the effort and care I provided him never seemed to be the right thing to do.

When I became pregnant with Junior, I was very proud of myself, proud that I was carrying a life inside of me and proud that I considered myself to be an adult who had someone to love, and someone who would love me. Junior was a good kid until his father left the household. Then he became a handful. After his dad and I split, he lived impulsively, wanted to do things his way, and he challenged the rules of the house. As Junior grew, we butted heads a lot. I established house rules and he broke the rules I had established by doing what he wanted to do.

When Junior was ten, I awoke one night with him sitting next to my bed with a pile of papers and a lighter, trying to start a fire. At first, I thought what I was seeing was a joke and I could not believe my eyes. Once I realized what I was seeing was real, I was horrified. My horror turned to anger and, after I had beat his butt, I realized he needed help, so we went to counseling. Counseling seemed to help a little, but I was still cautious and felt ill at ease around him. It was akin to waiting for the other shoe to drop. I no longer looked at Junior as an innocent little human being I had brought into the world.

After years of battles with Junior, things came to a head when at fourteen, he decided he was no longer going to school. Frustrated, angry, fearful I had lost control of the situation, tired of the constant battles, and almost to the breaking point, I laid down the law. "Either go to school or find your way out of my home." He chose to leave, and was picked up by the police. Sitting before the DA, I was filled with anger, disgust, fear, and despair, yet hopeful I could get some relief from my home situation. The DA informed me I could not throw my child out of the house at fourteen. I informed the DA that I worked two to three jobs, had two other children to provide for, and that I was not able to impress upon this child that he should go to school. The DA did not seem to have any sympathy for my plight because he informed me if I threw my son out of the house again, I would be locked up. This statement further infuriated me because I knew I had done all I could to make the situation at home better, and here I was being told, with no offer of a solution for my dilemma, that I had no choice but to let this individual remain disruptive to the household. So I retorted, "well then you can take care of the other two." The DA and I locked eyes. He repeated he would lock me up if this incident occurred again. I fired back with, "you can take care of the other two then." When the meeting with the DA concluded, I walked out of the DA's office almost in tears, not knowing what I was going to do to make the situation better or how I was going to cope with my inner turmoil and feelings of despair. As I was walking down the hall, I got stopped by an individual from an agency for troubled youth. He offered to take Junior off my hands for a few days and I accepted with relief and gratitude.

For a week, I had a peaceful home. No sibling fights and no deliberate attempts to challenge the household rules. And then that dreaded call came. I needed to pick up Junior. I waylaid the inevitable as long as I could by waiting until I was threatened by the agency with being reported to the police for child neglect. After picking him up, he returned to school and a teacher was able to talk him into finishing the ninth grade. On one hand, I was proud of him and full of hope that this would be a turning point in his way of thinking, being and doing as well as in our relationship. On the other hand, I had become somewhat numb and detached from Junior as a way of self-preservation.

When the school term started, again Junior seemed to adjust to returning to school. However, this was short lived. I came home one day, inquiring where Junior was, but no one knew or would admit that they knew. I checked all over the house and finally found him huddled under a blanket in the attic. I called his name and he would not respond. Feeling exasperated and not understanding why he was hiding in the attic or what, if anything, I could do, I said, "I didn't tell you to go up into the attic so I'm not telling you to come down." I closed the attic door and walked away. Figuring at least if he was hiding in the attic, I could have a little peace because I didn't have to interact with him directly. Finally, after a couple of days, I came home and there he sat in the dining room. Gathering up my courage and searching for just the right thing to do and say, I said to him, "oh, you finally decided to come out of the attic," and reminded him of my expectations that he go to school or get a job. Nothing changed, and just before I hit my breaking point, Russell stepped in and offered to give him work. There wasn't much pay, but at least it kept him out of mischief quite a bit of time and the household could maintain a peaceful environment. There were still incidences when my patience was tried, like when he set fire to the kitchen, deliberately broke things, such as my brand new, five-hundred dollar color television, and pestering of his sister. Junior's aversion to obeying household rules continued until his eighteenth birthday. I was so happy we had gotten to this point in both our lives and that I could initiate a new set of house rules that had enforcement consequences.

At 12:01 a.m. on the day of his birthday, I pulled out my whistle and ran through the house blowing it. This was my attempt at taking my life back. I was through putting up with this individual who had become an albatross around my neck, one I was unable to extricate myself from until now. The more I blew the whistle, the more powerful I felt. When I stopped blowing the whistle, I informed Junior he was now eighteen, and I asked him what his plans were since he could not stay here in this house with no job. I got no reply but I was not deterred because I knew that if he did not try to help himself, I would be free of him. Needless to say, nothing changed, and he decided he would not follow house rules and walked out the door. I was relieved, and decided not to worry because I could rest my nerves and I would have some peace.

I didn't see him for a while, but I was not totally concerned. I knew he was stubborn and smart enough to make a way for himself. True enough, because one day he showed up and gave me his GED diploma and announced he was going into the Navy. I congratulated him and thought he was finally putting his life on track. He went into the Navy and was discharged because he was diagnosed with paranoid schizophrenia. So back under my roof, he came and my nightmare with him started all over again. I did not understand the full ramifications of his sickness; I only knew I felt hopeless, exhausted, agitated, and put upon by this individual. Although I kept trying to reach him, I only seemed to get through to him when he was taking his medication. Knowing he was ill, I no longer pressed him about work. I only asked that he clean up behind himself and take a bath. At three hundred plus pounds, the stench of his body was more than I could tolerate. I always believed that someday, in some way, he would either become completely well or would be able to manage his illness, but watching him deteriorate from a person to a shell of a person made me very sad, fearful, and feeling helpless, yet hopeful that he could lead a normal life. In trying to find a solution for his predicament, I turned to a psychic for help. I took him for several readings, which seemed to bolster his spirits and it helped me cope with the situation. However, it did nothing to change the household dynamics. He was still off-kilter in his thinking, hearing voices, not taking his medication, and smelling up the house. So our cycle of ostrich-like stubbornness on both our parts ensued and out the door he would go, ending up wherever the money in his pocket would take him. The funny thing is wherever he landed, when things got really rough for him, he would always go to the VA hospital for help. They put him back on his meds and when he started doing better, released him to my care. I lost track of the number of times this scenario played out.

I LOVE YOU, I JUST DON'T LIKE YOU

One of the most devastating experiences with Junior happened one night after I had used a week's leave to go pick him up from the Florida VA hospital. Everything was going well for a short time. Junior was taking his medication and keeping himself clean. Things changed when I came home from work one evening and that familiar body odor greeted me at the front door. Even though I knew the answer, I questioned Junior about his bathing habits. He would not answer me and stormed off to his room with me right behind him. I noticed a change in his behavior, even though he took his bath without complaint. After that, I paid closer attention to Junior and saw he no longer smiled or participated with family members. He had become distant, brooding, and the familiar body odor was inching its way back into every room of the house. This behavior led me to believe he was off his meds, so we started having our usual dispute about them, and about bathing. This went on for about a week. One evening, after adamantly refusing my request, he suddenly stood up and looked at me. He said, "I wish you weren't my mother. I'm from Satan. You are from God. I'm from dad, and I just wish you weren't my mother." At this point, I didn't care to try and analyze what he meant because my feelings were too hurt. All I could say to him before going to my room to cry was, "from this moment on I am not his mother." I fled to my room, got in bed, and poured my heart out through tears. It seemed no matter how hard I tried to make things right, to keep peace in my family and do the best I could this individual whom I had taken care of and who had for the better part of his life been hard to digest had turned against me. After crying until I felt drained with no tears or emotions left, I looked up and asked, "Lord, what do I do now?" A voice answered, "take him to his father". Not knowing exactly where that might be, I called my ex sister-in-law and explained that Junior needed to see his father and asked if she would be kind enough to give me his address. I explained I wasn't asking for money or anything, just that his son needed to touch base with him. To my relief, she gave me the address. I took off from work early the next day, gathered a friend, my middle child, Russell and Junior, and drove to the address I had been given. Relief flooded through me when Sylvester opened the door because I knew this was my chance to be free of Junior's burden and where, come what may, I was going to leave his and my child. I informed him I had his son and I was leaving Junior with him. He stepped outside of the door, looked at Junior and said, "take him back, take him back to his mother." He turned and started walking towards his door with me and his son following, still loudly saying, "take him back to his mother." As we reached his door, I finally said, "I am his mother." That took him aback for a moment and then he continued with, "he can't stay here, so take him back with you." Our son walked up to him and said, "dad, it's me, I'm your son," to which Sylvester replied, "I don't care, go back with your mother."

His father telling him that, walking into his house, and shutting the door behind him seemed to send Junior over the edge. Before I could finish unloading the car with his things, Junior dropped the belongings he had in his hand and ran past me towards a major intersection. My passengers and I picked up his things, got in the car, and drove in the direction he had run to. By the time we reached him, we saw him lying in the middle of a major intersection with arms outstretched. People had gathered around him and were trying to get him out of the way of traffic. My passengers and I stayed in the car and watched as he was led to the sidewalk out of the street. I did not know what else to do other than to leave him. I could not take another round of dispute with him. I was way too exhausted to put any more effort into Junior's well-being. I decided to head home and leave him as he was. I needed the mental break or I was going to have a breakdown. Knowing his pattern of going to the VA hospital when he was in trouble, I felt he would either go there or get his father to change his mind. At that point, I just didn't have the strength to care about his welfare. I found out later he had gone to the VA hospital. After getting back on his medication, he apologized to me and never mentioned his father again. By this time I felt I loved this person, I just did not like him, so his apology meant very little to me. It was hard to make peace with my home situation. I felt I had no safe, peaceful haven. I felt heavily burdened, with no way out. I felt like, at the end of each day, I had to endure someone I would rather not look at, at all. I felt guilty because I wanted to be free of my flesh and blood. I felt as though I had nowhere to turn. I felt like a failure because everything I had tried to do to make things better had failed. I felt trapped into taking care of someone who should be living on their own and taking care of themselves. I felt ashamed for feeling the way I did. I wanted the agony I was feeling to stop. I wanted my son to be permanently put in an institution, but could not make this happen. I agonized over my situation so often, the pain I felt seemed normal. I had no respite. I could not run away because I still had a child to prepare for adulthood. I could not cry because I was in too much pain. All I could do was fearfully go through the motions of living and hope that my agony would be over soon.

MY AGONY IS FINALLY OVER

Whenever Junior was in the VA hospital, I felt relief. Relief in knowing he was safe and being taken care of. I was relieved to be free of the constant tug of war with him. Junior returned to the VA psyche ward and I began to feel free from stress when the VA hospital called to say they were releasing him. I begged them not to release him because I felt he was not ready to be released based on the conversation I had with him earlier. I was informed they could not hold him any longer. Even though I felt frustrated, angry, tired, and near despair, I agreed to pick him up in a couple of days. I felt I needed that time to gather my patience and courage to undergo another round of battle of the wills with him.

When I spoke to Junior, I did not realize it was the last time I would speak with him. For some reason, I felt the need to tell him I loved him in addition to the day and time I could pick him up. Instead of waiting for me he signed himself out of the hospital. He left the hospital walking towards who knows where on a cold December day with very little clothes on. Trying to make sure he would return to the VA, I went to the bank, but I was too late; he had withdrawn all of his funds. I resigned myself that he was in the wind, so to speak, which meant he would be able to take care of his immediate needs and I would have a peaceful home until I got another phone call from him saying, "come and get me."

The call that came late one night was not the call I was expecting. The call came from the police asking me if I knew Junior. I replied he was my son, and the officer informed me Junior had "expired". It took me a moment to understand what the police officer was saying because I had never heard the expression of "expiring" as a way of saying someone had died. I called Annie and learned that Andy, my youngest, was with her and we all went to the morgue to identify Junior. It was a quiet ride back to my house after the morgue identification, each of us lost in thought and not knowing what to say. Since Junior's demise, we rarely, if ever, talk about him. I don't know why, my best guess is there's nothing left to say. We are left with our memory of him and for me, that's enough. I do not care to dredge up old memories of Junior's antics or remember the zombie-like person he turned into. I choose to hold a memory of him as a vibrant human being, arguing with his brother about a Redskin game or giving a handout to someone in need. I choose to hold onto the memory that even with all of his folly, he loved me.

For a while after Junior died, I walked around dazed, just doing the bare minimum that needed to be done. The worst was

94

seeing guys on the street that looked like Junior. On numerous occasions, I almost approached the person to see if he was in any condition to have a sensible conversation, but would catch myself and remember that my son was gone and that the individual I saw before me was not him. I was torn between missing the person who was kind-hearted and caring and who could make me laugh when he was on his medication, to the person who was argumentative, stubborn, stank up the whole house with his body odor, and had difficulty living a life of purpose. I took solace in the fact that I didn't have to worry about him any longer, that the last words I had said to him was that I loved him.

But I was also relieved that my constant struggle with him was finally over. I used to be cautious in how I expressed to other people the gratitude I felt in knowing that Junior had passed on into a peaceful state, which ended our time together. I knew most people would not understand my feeling of relief instead of grief because, even today, when anyone asked me about family and I mentioned that Junior died, I get a response of, "oh, you poor thing". In truth, I feel like it was a blessed thing, not a poor one, because I no longer have to fight for my sanity. I no longer care what others think when I say I am glad he has gone on. I lived through the madness of coping with a paranoid schizophrenic individual.

I once felt ashamed to admit my son was a paranoid schizophrenic. I felt his sickness somehow reflected on me as a person and on my parenting skills. It took a long time after he died to come to terms with the feelings of lowliness associated with bringing an individual into this world who had this type of illness. I was not able to talk about Junior's illness with others other than to vent about his antics. It was not until I investigated the illness that I was able to make peace with myself. I learned the illness was brought to light by Junior's Navy tour of duty.

I am sure there are other factors, but the point is, I was able to make peace with myself because I didn't have to continue to blame myself for Junior's disease. No, I don't blame the Navy. I don't blame anyone or anything. I may not understand why Junior developed the illness, but what I do know is that everything happens for a reason and everything we experience in our lives happens on a path to learning to love. I struggled with Junior for years and at times, I felt very alone, desperate for help, and near my breaking point. The only thing that kept me sane was what I call an expiration date. I knew that, at some point, my trials and tribulations would be over because everything or every situation we find ourselves in has an end date attached. Even during the darkest times, I fervently held onto the hope that my struggle would end peacefully with Junior, either getting well or permanently placed in an institution where he could be properly taken care of. Unless you have lived with someone and struggled for years as you watch them turn from a vibrant human being to a soulless, walking zombie, then you might be hard-pressed to understand when I say I am glad that part of my life is over.

What I learned from a mentally incarcerated child was that blame and guilt are like burdensome twins, but through forgiveness, they cannot exist. A major part of being a parent lies in forgiving our offspring. We, as human beings, are taught that in order to be forgiven of our own transgressions, we must forgive others of theirs. I would like to add an addendum to that thought, as it is applies to parenthood. Being a parent means letting go of our offspring when we have reached a point in our development where we no longer wish to constantly feel bad about our children's treatment of us, or we evolve to the realization that we have nothing left to give to our children. I believe we do not need to walk around feeling wounded because someone attacks us verbally or blatantly disregards our feelings; this is especially true when it comes to our children. No one stops having feelings, their own demons, or inner turmoil because they have become a parent. Yet, we may consistently disregard or sacrifice our own needs or bury hurt feelings in response to our adult children. How often do we forgive ourselves for any hurt or wrongdoing, we may have knowingly or unknowingly inflicted on our kids? Chances are we rarely, if ever, forgive ourselves. Instead, our bad feelings get pushed down deep inside and eventually turn to guilt and then to physical pain. If you carry any feelings of guilt or shame concerning your children, you can be free of these feelings by first understanding that you are/were the best parent you could be based on what you knew while raising your children. Second, you can take comfort in the knowledge that being a parent means you are above all, a human being who has earned the right to have peace of mind, and to live a life free of any frustration or discomfort that may be inflicted upon you by your descendants.

Sometimes as a parent, we yearn to be free of our children because of the tremendous burdens placed on our shoulders by our children, society, and ourselves. Our inner turmoil and external obligations may leave very little of our true essence remaining in the quest to raise self-sufficient children. Once our children become adults, we get into mental trouble in continuing a posture that served us well when they were young, but does nothing for us when they reach adulthood. Sometimes it doesn't even dawn on us we haven't accepted the fact that our once dependent urchins are now self-sufficient adults prone to live in ways we find distasteful.

As human beings, we personally experience numerous ups and downs, causing us to pause while we re-gather our strength. We, parents, live with daunting tasks fraught with numerous pitfalls in which the answer to a problem may not be readily discernable. In addition to parenting, we have to fight with our own inner demons, environmental turmoil, and ever-present fears. What parents need to remember is our decisions are based on what we believe to be the most viable solution to a problem at the time the problem occurred, and to forgive ourselves if a choice turned out differently than we intended it to.

GUILT AND SHAME

Guilt and shame are cut from the same cloth. Both entice you to feel bad about yourself. Guilt happens when you have feelings of remorse and regret. You feel sorry about something and you want to make amends.

Shame, on the other hand, is an emotion that is more harmful than guilt because it eats away at our self-esteem. You feel pain and humiliation and sorrow for being who you are.

Both guilt and shame can be detrimental to our very existence when we harbor bad feelings about things we did or decisions we made based on what we knew at the time. We cannot return to that time or place where it made sense to us to do the thing we feel so wretched about now. Guilt and shame usually follows could have, should have, and would have thoughts. In other words, I would have done this if the other person did that, I should have done something and because I didn't something that should not have occurred, did, I could have done this or that but I chose another way. Guilt and shame can only exist when you allow thoughts about things, circumstances, and events to fester.

I can't say we can live without guilt or shame, but I can say we can side step their effects on our life. We can do this by understanding we are human and prone to make mistakes, and that the best cure for guilt and shame is forgiveness. The key to alleviating or releasing guilt or shame is to forgive yourself for allowing a person or circumstance to take you to a place within that caused you to act in an unloving way. One of the most powerful lessons I ever learned was not to accept as mine the guilty and shameful actions of another. My husband taught this lesson to me.

After a couple years of marriage, I was contacted by social services and asked if my brother could live with me. I don't recall how they found me, but I was elated to be asked to assume responsibility for him. My husband agreed to allow him to live with us and, for about two weeks, everything went well. My brother attended school and obeyed house rules and my husband brought home the bacon. I don't know why my husband started badgering my brother and trying to pick physical fights with him, but it became an everyday thing. I was unable to stop the abuse from my husband towards my brother, so my brother left my home. I felt terrible. I was caught between a rock and a hard place. My husband was the only means of support for the family and my brother was someone I wanted desperately to help. I felt ashamed and guilt-ridden because I was unable to protect my brother from my husband. I also felt at fault and responsible for his leaving my home.

Years later, after my marriage had ended, I ran into my brother on the street. I was ecstatic to see him and we spent a short time catching up. When I learned he needed a place to stay, I jumped at the chance to help him, and invited him to live with my children and me. Even though I was on public assistance at the time and had very little, I was happy to finally have the opportunity to make up as best I could for not being able to protect him earlier. My brother said he was a barber and went to work every day, but I did not ask him for financial help because I was too intent on making up for the past. Soon he asked if his girlfriend could spend a few nights and I agreed. The few nights turned into two weeks and my home started feeling crowded. Within a short time after his girlfriend moved in, I noticed money started disappearing from my purse. At first, half of what was in my wallet would be gone and then every dime I had went missing. I suspected my brother was taking the money and questioned him about it. He admitted he was stealing from me because he needed bus fare. I tried being understanding, but started hiding my purse. He found it anyway, no matter where I hid it in my room. After he took my last dime for the third time, I'd had enough and asked him to leave.

What I learned from the relationship with my brother was that could have, should have, and would have got me again. I overlooked my brother's actions in favor of relieving my guilt and shame. I felt ashamed I had not been in a position to assist my brother earlier. I felt guilty because I had not found a way to keep

99

my brother in the household during my marriage. I realized I had taken on the responsibility for my husband's actions as if his actions were my own. I believed it was my fault my husband had treated my brother so badly. I felt like a failure. None of which was true.

Responsibility for another means to have control over someone. I had no control over my husband's actions. My husband was the person who belittled and picked fights with my brother, I didn't. Because I was not in a financial position to better assist my brother, I took on the burden of shame and guilt. What I didn't realize at the time is that you can't help someone else if you can't help yourself. I felt as though I should have somehow forced my husband to treat my brother better even though I had no idea how to accomplish this. I allowed could have, should have, and would have thoughts to run rampant within my mind, rendering me incapable of getting a clear picture of the situation. "Could have" told me it was my fault my husband was mistreating my brother. "Should have" told me I should have tried harder to maintain peace in the home. "Would have" told me I should have found a way to make things better for my brother.

Over time, as I realized I was carrying my husband's weight, I began to understand his actions were his karma, not mine. When I did not comprehend my connection to the situation, it felt as though I was receiving my husband's punishment while he walked around unscathed. Once I realized I was holding onto something that did not belong to me, shame and guilt miraculously disappeared along with their predecessors could have, should have, and would have.

When I was employed as an administrative assistant, I worked for a guy who called my name incessantly, pushed me into upgrading my skills, and gave me cash awards and promotions without my having to ask for them. To brighten up the office, I brought in a plant one day but could not find a suitable place for it in the outer office, so I asked my employer if I could place it in his office. He agreed to keep it in his office and I agreed to take care of it. Our agreement worked well for quite a while. I tended to the plant's care and it responded by growing well. That is, until the organization was reorganized. During the reorganization, I was assigned a new supervisor. When I tried to retrieve the plant, my present supervisor told me I could not have it. At first, I thought he was joking, but once I realized he was serious, I became angry that he was arbitrarily taking something that was rightfully mine. I was determined to get my plant back. It was not that I would not have given him the plant had he asked, or not insisted on keeping it, but he didn't ask. He just took. I felt he was disregarding my rights and therefore did not deserve the plant, so I waited until he went to lunch and retrieved it then.

I felt torn between two opposing emotions. On one hand, I felt bad because I had to resort to such measures to retrieve something I considered rightfully mine from someone who had helped me. On the other hand, I felt anger towards the supervisor and justified in my actions. I carried these mixed emotions until I ran into that supervisor in the building snack bar. While waiting in line to pay for my coffee, I heard a familiar voice, ranting and raving. As I turned around, I came face to face with my former supervisor and was greeted with, "you think you something cause you work for the assistant secretary. You think you something now, don't you?" Over and over he loudly repeated these words. I was embarrassed to share the same air with him. I turned, placed the coffee money on the counter, and fled the snack bar, all the while praying I would never have to see him again. Not only was I embarrassed, but I also felt responsible for his tirade. It wasn't until many years later I realized the responsibility for the way he acted was not mine. He was the person who chose to react the way he did. It occurred to me that if there were any shame or guilt to be had, it wasn't mine. It was reserved for the person committing the action.

FEAR, FRIEND OR FOE

Fear keeps us focused on the past or worried about
the future. If we can acknowledge our fear, we can
realize that right now we are okay. Right now, today,
we are still alive, and our bodies are working
marvelously. Our eyes can still see the beautiful sky.
Our ears can still hear the voices of our loved ones.
Thich Nhat Hanh

Have you ever been afraid of fear? I have. Not only did I feel
fearful, I feared feeling fearful. I did not recognize that below the
surface of my fearful emotion lay a multitude of fears. Whenever I
allowed fear to rule my life, I felt stuck in a time warp of inactivity
in which I was unable to make a decision or move beyond self-
imposed boundaries. There was my fear of what others will say, fear
of success, fear of failure, fear of not being good enough, fear of
wanting too much, fear of moving too fast, fear of moving too slow,
just to name a few. I felt helpless and torn between wanting to do
something but unable to do anything because my mind kept telling
me I was in danger of making the wrong decision. Get the picture? I
was so acutely steeped in fear that I feared fear itself.

It took me many years to recognize how much I depended on
fear to keep me entrenched in self-doubt and anxiety. It was not until
I felt stuck in life, as though I was repeating the same situations with
the same types of individuals, that I had an ah hah moment. I
reached a point where I was drowning in memories of the past and
felt unable to move forward. I had hit my brick wall. That is, I
became downright tired of living in a fear-laden state of mind. Once
I became tired of being overwhelmed by my fear, I made the
decision to face my fears head on. I stopped watching the news
because it fed me a constant diet of bad things about my
environment. According to the news reports, whatever was
happening in the environment around me was beyond my control.
The only thing I was doing was becoming depressed about world
events and life struggles. I stopped listening to constant complainers

because their presence brought down my spirit. I looked around my home and, out loud, thanked God for everything he had given me right down to the minutest object I had in my possession. While driving, I thanked God I was driving on pavement instead of dirt, for traffic lights, for lines on the road, and stop signs that kept me safe. I thanked God for anything and everything I could think of. It was then I began to understand everything, even fear, had a purpose in my life.

Knowing fear will always exist within us, it is unrealistic to believe we can live fearlessly because our five senses constantly input stimulus to our brain. Since getting away from fear is impossible, what is our next option? I would venture to say we have to live with it. What we don't have to live with is fear's crippling effects on our lives.

Fear is one of the most powerful emotions anyone can experience. It carries with it a response to the environment in which we either take flight or stay and fight. Can fear be a friend? Yes, it can. It is a friend when it stops you from hurting yourself or someone else. It is your friend when it stops you from committing a crime. It is your friend when it helps you out of a dangerous situation. It is your friend when it propels you into action when you have hit your "brick wall".

Fear is not a friend when you allow it to stifle your growth from becoming the person you were meant to be, or when you live in bondage to your emotions, become paralyzed into inaction, causing you to settle for the known, when you become paranoid in your thinking by seeing danger in every facet of life, when you stop trusting your own instinct and accept another's ideas about your life because of your past mistakes, if you remain in a hurtful situation, feeling as though you are damned if you do and damned if you don't, or if you feel compelled to say nothing about things that hurt you. And last but not least, when used in conjunction with could have, should have, or would have, it is a destroyer of inner peace, resulting in an inability to go beyond the crazy eight or see saw pattern.

A lot of my fear centered on failing at something and the imagined shame or disgrace associated with the failure. Now, in moments of fear, I recite the two definitions of fear: "Forget everything and run, or face everything and rise. The choice is yours," author unknown. I use these two definitions as a reminder to not allow fear to rule my life as it has done for so many years.

IT JUST AIN'T WHAT I THOUGHT IT WOULD BE

Once I completed stenography school, I went to work for the federal government because I believed the organization helped others in a fair and equal way. I was thrilled at being hired mainly based on my entry-level test scores, and I envisioned myself working my way to the top rather quickly. It did not take me long to realize the government is just as cutthroat as any other entity. I discovered that people stabbed each other in the back and, if you were part of an up and coming clique, you made out very well. My employment with the federal government was a big disappointment to me. I was never able to balance my concept of how I thought the federal government should operate with how the federal government actually operated.

Not only did the federal government employ me in a civilian capacity, but I also joined the U.S. Army Reserve. It was hard work until I became an instructor. As an instructor, I discovered a new talent: I could learn written material overnight. I also discovered I enjoyed sharing what I learned in creative ways the next day.

Working with the U.S. Army Reserves afforded me the opportunity to learn new skills, discover hidden talents, earn extra income, and provided me a reprieve from parenting. It also provided me with an extra paid vacation of seventeen days each year. I felt like I had found Nirvana because I was doing something I was good at and that I was completely loyal to. Even though Reserve duty was slated to be one weekend a month, I usually worked three due to student recruiting from other branches of the military.

I loved being in the military for fourteen years, but it lost its fascination and appeal when they decided to dump me. Being dumped by the military made me feel used and desolate, and all my old feelings of worthlessness, abandonment, anxiety, and fear resurfaced after hearing I was no longer acceptable to the military. I had been an excellent soldier, did everything I was asked to do, and had put my heart and soul into fulfilling my soldierly duties. I was told that because I had been instructing for eight years, I could no longer teach, that I had to find a new home. After being told by the first sergeant I wasn't good enough to run an office, I took a long look at the military.

Once the initial shock began to wear off, I found myself reverting to the familiar pattern of going into my room, closing the door, and talking to the air. I regaled my virtues of being an outstanding military leader starting with a story of what should have happened to a good soldier such as myself. I told myself what could happen if I remained a soldier, and I reminded myself that, if the military would only listen to me and review my outstanding record, all would be well. I almost drove myself crazy with could have, should have, and would have thoughts. I had to find a way to let go of the military, or else lose me. It took a while, but I was finally able to release my mental association with the military. As I worked through my hurt feelings, I realized the military no longer held value for me and I felt as though I had been living under a veil of delusion. I reminisced about all the times I had devoted to the military's cause, the pride I felt in doing something I considered significant. I thought about the awards of excellence I had received for doing a good job, I thought about the devotion to military duty, I thought about the countless hours I had put into serving or completing a given task. All these thoughts took on a different meaning once I was told I was no longer needed to contribute to something I found fulfilling. Suddenly, I felt like a fool who had lived under the delusion that the military took care of its own, that if you performed the task you were given and obeyed the military's rules, you would remain a viable resource. I felt heartbroken, betrayed, and abandoned, so I decided I'd had enough. I walked away from the military and never looked back.

DECIDING TO HEAL

"Nobody can hurt me without my
permission." Mahatma Gandhi

Deciding to be better or feel better about yourself is the first step to
healing your inner turmoil. The next step is to decide what to choose
to heal. Here are some examples. I choose to feel whole and
healthy. I choose to forgive my offspring and to let go of them. I
choose to no longer feel abandoned by my children. I choose to let
go of the shame and guilt associated with my significant others. I
choose to respect my feelings as well as my offspring's choice to be
as they choose to be. I choose, I choose, I choose. The optimum
words here are "I choose", because in order to begin to feel whole,
you need to choose to feel better.

I learned through experience, and sometimes had to
re-learn, there comes a time in life when you have to either
sink or swim. What I mean is you can continue down the
painful path you're on, or stop, take inventory of how you
got there, and then step out in a new direction. The
decisions I had to make were not always easy, but they
were necessary for my self-preservation and for my
family's well-being. Whenever I reached what I call my
pinnacle of pain, the point of no return, "*I choose*," always
came into play in my life because I had to make a decision
to either go forward or remain on a painful path.

"A carter was driving a wagon along a country lane when the
wheels sank down deep into a rut. The rustic driver, stupefied and
aghast, stood looking at the wagon and did nothing but utter loud
cries to Hercules to come and help him. Hercules, it is said, appeared
and addressed him thus: "Put your shoulders to the wheels, my man.
Goad on your bullocks, and never more pray to me for help until you
have done your best to help yourself, or depend upon it, you will
henceforth pray in vain."" Aesop

Most of us carry pain buried deep inside from hurts inflicted on us by the people who were supposed to love and protect us. When we carry old hurts in this way, once we are adults, the hurts have become an intrinsic part of who we believe we are. We develop numerous ways to circumvent the pain, and we contend the pain is our parent's fault. In turn, we abuse others and ourselves because we blame people for our own actions. If we find ourselves in a bad situation, we say because we were taught by our parents to react a certain way, it is their fault. We blame our parents because they did not give us, so we think, the proper tools to survive in life. We blame our parents because we feel we were wrongfully punished into submitting to a way of thinking that caused us to make wrong choices in our lives. We blame our parents for not giving us enough attention as children so we seek constant attention from others at any cost. We blame our parents because they did not make enough money to buy us everything we wanted, which caused us to feel deprived. We never stop to think that our parents are human beings who are or were the walking, wounded people who did the best they knew how to raise us. We seek only to blame them for who we are and what we have become. How many times have we said to ourselves "this is the way I was taught so I have to continue along this path"? We become embroiled in avoidance of the pain by allowing ourselves to continue to drift in the very direction that makes us uncomfortable.

As adults, we cannot continue blaming our parents because we choose to hold onto the pain experienced as children from methods used to help us reach adulthood. When we blame our parents in this way, they assume the role of our personal crutch. Thoughts centered on what our parents could have, should have, or would have done become the catalyst to the emotional traumas we continue to experience. This means whenever something goes astray in our lives, we revert to an emotional state in which we believe our parents are at the root cause of the issue. Continuing to blame our parents for who we are as adults gives our personal power (our inner strength and sense of purpose) away to the very people we are blaming. In the final analysis, we are the captains of our ship. As such, we must steer our own course, regardless of the obstacles encountered.

"There is an expiry date on blaming your parents for steering you in the wrong direction. The moment you are old enough to take the wheel, the responsibility lies with you." J. K. Rowling

TOO MUCH PARENTING

One of the hardest things a parent has to do is release their offspring into adulthood. We may believe they are not mature enough to take care of themselves and therefore still pursue the role of caretaker. What we fail to realize is that if we continue to stay totally engrossed in their lives, we have done a disservice not only to our children, but also to ourselves.

Think about it. Have you allowed your children to exercise their right to be an individual, even if it means they don't seem to care about you? Have you granted them the courtesy of acceptance of their posture in life? Have you gotten over the fear that you did something that fit with should have, could have, and would have? Are you fighting with yourself for feeling the way you do about your children? Are you terrified that the grown up child will walk away from you, leaving you in a situation you have no control over? Do you actually care about your offspring? Have you allowed your children to torment you? Have you tried to fit your children into a mold you created for them? Do your children feel like an albatross around your neck? Are you fighting with your children? Do you mind your children's business to the point of interference? Is there mutual respect between your children and you? Are you drawn to drama with your children? Have we allowed ourselves to become our children's punching ball? Have you allowed your children to grow up? Have you allowed your children to find their own way in life or did you set a course and expect them to follow the course you set? Do you allow your children to disrespect you in some way? Have you tried to communicate with your loved one, only to find they want nothing to do with you? Is it hard to accept your children just as they are? Do you hide your belongings when your child comes over because the child has sticky fingers? Are you afraid to make a move without consulting your child first? Have you given your child control of your life? Do you honestly like the person you raised? Does the air feel like electrical currents running through it when your child comes to visit?

If you can answer "yes" to any of these questions, it is time to re-evaluate, take stock of the situation, and decide if this is how you want to continue to live. If you want or need to change the dynamics between you and your offspring, first choose to change yourself, because change starts with you. Next decide what your boundaries will be in the relationship--what feels comfortable to you (you may need to meditate on this one). Put your boundaries in place and stick to your guns.

On the other hand, you may feel your child owes you because you supported him or her when they were unable to support themselves. Think about this for a moment. Does your child really owe you something other than respectful interaction? No, because it is not mandatory that a child love a parent. It is our children's decision to love us, just as it is our decision to love them. We choose to be loving and supportive parents. We choose to foster the health and well-being of our offspring until they reach adulthood. These are choices we make as parents because we want our children to grow up to be self-sufficient, loving adults. If you live under the guise that your child is supposed to take care of you because you have reached a point in your life that you cannot take care of yourself, think again. Your child does not owe you love. Love gives without expecting a return. Love does not do something for someone else while expecting something in return for what was given. Count your blessings if your child has reached a point in their maturity where they lovingly interact with you and assist you. Just remember, it is the child's decision to do so because he or she chooses to do so, and it is a child's decision to love us just as it is our decision to love them. We are not here to demand that our children do something for us, or to love us.

If we still blame our parents for who we are, we cannot expect our youngsters to miraculously not place blame on us for whatever issue they may be experiencing in life. The idiom, *"you can only give what you have to give"*, personifies my point. All of the ideas, mores and values our parents imparted to us, will be passed along to our children unless we have made a conscious effort to root out the negative emotional damage left over from childhood. If we have not healed our emotional wounds by forgiving our parent's transgressions, our children will mirror our emotional wounds by acting in ways that cause us grief. Our thinking, in turn, will go to could have, should have, or would have, causing us to feel grief, pain, and shame.

TAKING A LOOK AT THE ROOT CAUSE OF PAIN

As parents, we often look back at the times we shared with our children. Most of the time, we regret some action we took in response to a situation or circumstance. Our mind brings our attention back to what we think we could have done, should have done, or would have done differently in reaction to a situation or circumstance.

A major part of being a parent lies in forgiving our offspring. We, as human beings, are taught that to be forgiven of our own transgressions, we must forgive others of theirs. I would like to add an addendum to that thought, as it is applied to parenthood. Being a parent means letting go of our offspring when we reach a point in our development where we no longer wish to constantly feel bad about our children's treatment of us, or we evolve to the realization that we have nothing left to give to our children. I believe we do not need to walk around feeling wounded because someone else verbally attacked us or blatantly disregarded our feelings, especially in relation to our children. No one stops having feelings, their own demons, or inner turmoil because they have become a parent. Yet, we may consistently disregard or sacrifice our own needs or bury hurt feelings in response to our adult children's needs. How often do we forgive ourselves for any hurt or wrongdoing we may have knowingly or unknowingly inflicted on our kids? Chances are we

111

rarely, if ever, forgive ourselves. Instead, our bad feelings get pushed down deep inside and eventually turn to guilt, shame, and then to physical pain. If you carry inside you any feelings of guilt or shame concerning your children, you can be free of these feelings by first understanding that you are/were the best parent you could be based on what you knew while raising your children. Second, you can take comfort in the knowledge that being a parent means you are, above all, a human being who has earned the right to have peace of mind, and to live a life free of any frustration or discomfort that may be inflicted upon you by your descendants.

In a weakened or exhaustive state of parenthood, you will do things just to keep peace. You will go against your better judgment to make a person happy, even though happiness can be fleeting and usually is in these circumstances. All the while, you will suffer inside and put yourself down because of guilt, or shame, or feeling like the pawn of a human being you delivered into this world. You might be asking yourself "what am I talking about?" and asking the question, "isn't that what parents are supposed to do?" I used to feel a parent had to maintain a relationship with their children at all costs and always harbored guilt feelings. If you feel being the parent of an adult individual requires you to always sacrifice who you are for the sake of being a part of the individual's life, then the hurt, anger, and disappointment you feel will remain a part of your daily existence.

If you are a parent who reared your child to be an adult to the best of your ability only to find yourself caught up in some horrific experiences you never imagined possible, maybe it's time to let go of the offender. I am talking about parents who have children strung out on drugs and who have tried to help them, over and over. I am talking about parents who have children constantly incarcerated for either small or major crimes who have given their all in supporting their children, but to no avail. I am talking about parents who are now raising their grandchildren because their child can't or won't act like a parent to their own children. I am talking about the parents who find themselves being neglected because their grown children have better things to do. I am talking about parents who touched their inner being, only to find emptiness where there once was hope, who are or have sunk into despair and depression because their offspring can't germinate into an adult.

Yes, there are numerous parents who are repeatedly deceived by their offspring, or have taken up the gauntlet of caretaker for their grandchildren at a time when they would love to be able to have a life of their own. While I do not postulate washing your hands of your children completely, I do recommend that you think, really think, about the best option for maintaining your own sanity and well-being. Call it tough love if you must, but ask yourself, "are you helping you, or the person?" Ask yourself why you continue along the same path with the same results. And ask yourself if you are tired of feeling the way you do and of worrying yourself sick, of feeling ashamed, or carrying their weight on your shoulders, are you tired of living in regret, wondering when it will end, feeling guilty, and being hurt by someone who professes to love you? Now ask yourself, when will it stop? When is enough, enough?

Sometimes when you ask yourself these questions, you have to wade through dross and inner damage. This makes it very difficult to take an honest look at any situation and to develop or find an answer that will help you heal, but it can and must be done. To not look at a troubling situation in as honest a manner as you can means the continuance of inner and outer pain. The knowledge, enlightenment, and uplifting of your spirits that can be gained from self-examination has an immediate effect on your body. The adage, dis-ease brings disease, couldn't have expressed this cause and effect principle better. Understanding the principle of, "you can't help someone else if you can't help yourself" is apropos in dealing with your adult children. Know when it's time to let go of the cause of your misery, by listening to your insides and asking yourself what is the cause of the pain I feel?

REJECTION
Throughout my life, I have often felt rejected or cast aside. As a child, I felt rejected by my guardian whenever I tried to show

her love. As an adult, by my husband when he became an albatross around my neck instead of my supportive companion. By my daughter when she seemed to want to hurt me in some way at every turn. And by friends who betrayed me.

Rejection is not a pleasant feeling. It is not a feeling that nurtures you. It's the kind of feeling that tears at your soul and psyche, leaving you feeling sad and with low to no self-esteem. Rejection from another can take you inside yourself to a place where you feel totally worthless and leave you with a residue of depression. Rejection can take away your will to survive and with it, all sense of your reasons for living. Not understanding how or why I felt pain, a myriad of emotions always accompanied any feelings of rejection. It took some time for me to realize my feeling of rejection caused me to undergo the seesaw or crazy eight pattern of two emotions in direct opposite of each other taking turns activating and releasing each other within me.

Sometimes my crazy eight pattern consisted of my feeling helpless and sad, and when I would get tired of those feelings, I switched to feeling self-righteous indignation. When I got tired of self-righteous indignation, I would switch back to sadness and helplessness. Sound familiar? I was in this crazy eight pattern until I had an epiphany. It suddenly occurred to me I was acting contrary to what I wanted to be, peaceful and in harmony with myself, without the constant vacillation between emotional states. I began to recognize that I was not powerless or a pawn of my emotions. I began to seek a better way to deal with challenges that I faced. And so began my journey to self-acceptance, one that has taken me along the path of becoming a human being entitled to honor my feelings, not a space alien.

Rejection can also feel as though you have been dropped off in the middle of the desert without food, shelter, or water. It's as though you have no reprieve from scorching heat and can only suffer through it all. I have come to realize rejection is the first step to healing a part of me that I may or may not have realized needed healing. There have been times, when I felt disconnected from the human race. I have used various means to find relief from the internal conflicts that came with rejection. I tried finding relief through sex, long hours of sleep, alcohol (no, I didn't overindulge), self-pity, and I used rationalization to dull the pain I was experiencing. None of my relief methods worked until I made a conscious choice to remember that I did not have to continue carrying painful emotions around inside me because I was not someone else's "cup of tea". I am a human being, I am important, and by virtue of my being here on earth, I have value. Once I began to realize I have value, I decided to try affirmations as a way of getting to the root cause of my pain.

Doing affirmation exercises helped keep me balanced, and life took on new meaning for me. At first, it seemed silly to stand in front of a mirror, gently touching my throat and repeating, "I love and approve of myself just as I am". In the beginning, I could not bear to look into my eyes as I uttered these words, but I kept at it until I could look into my eyes without turning away and, within a short while, I felt good being me.

LETTING GO

Sometimes healing requires us to let go of another. When you let go of someone, you stop allowing thoughts about them be the central focus of your life. You stop regurgitating their memory. You allow yourself to step away from any involvement, mentally or physically, with the person. You make a conscious effort to forgive them. You feel free from the internal struggle associated with your relationship with the person. You release the fear of losing the person. You stop holding onto the need to have a relationship with the person

Letting go of someone you love can be one of the hardest things you ever have to do, but may be a necessary one. Before letting go of another, you can fret over how you, or things you experienced with the individual, would have turned out differently if things would have been done differently. You will recount all the things you enjoyed, got angry over, tried to fix, and loved doing with the person. You will imagine a certain someone's touch, feel, smell, and the way they looked at you. You may even try maintaining a dreamy illusory state of mind about a person because it becomes a way of getting through your loneliness, and because sometimes you just don't know how to let go.

This illusionary state may last for weeks, months, or years until you come to the realization that you have had enough. I call this hitting a brick wall. If you have hit a brick wall in your relationship with another and can find no way to have peaceful exchanges with the individual, set your intention to living free from the pain you are experiencing. Setting your intention to be free of internal pain starts your healing process. You can then begin to let go of a painful relationship. Once you have set your intention to live free from pain, begin to let go of the need to be needed by someone who is deliberately hurting you. Let go of the sorrow you feel because you can't have or don't have a relationship with this person. It is essential for you to understand that being in a relationship with someone requires two people, not just one. Why dwell on what might be, could be, or should be with a person? Because if a person is meant to be in your life, they will be, and not in a painful way either.

THE TANGLED WEB OF PAIN

"Most of our beliefs are generalizations about our past based on our interpretations of painful and pleasurable experiences. It's not the events of our lives that shape us, but our beliefs as to what those events mean. It's never the events of our lives, but the meaning we attach to the events and how we interpret them. Beliefs are designed to be a guiding force to tell us what will lead to pain and what will lead to pleasure. Beliefs play a major role in guiding our actions towards what would have, could have, and should have been. They help sustain us throughout our life." Tony Robbins. Sometimes we are so captivated by an idea (thought), and our emotion (feeling which influences our behavior) surrounding the thought, that we forget we travelled down the path of this thought pattern numerous times and got nowhere. Our beliefs take center stage causing our emotions to follow. Thoughts, beliefs, and emotions all play a part in our well-being. They are instrumental in our brain's function and the way the brain manages our life, because they assist the brain to change direction.

I hope you understand from reading this book that could have, should have, and would have are not conducive to a peaceful solution to any problem; thinking like this only makes things worse. I have come to realize that we exist on this earth to learn, grow, and fulfill our destiny. Being stuck in could have, should have, or would have keeps us in a single path in time with no way out. These thought patterns allow us to only see what was done in the past and to make us feel bad. Thoughts centered around could have, should have, and would have do not allow us to cross over onto any other path that will make us feel well. Instead, they leave us stuck in a time warp in which we are driven by emotions, thoughts, and feelings.

"Most of our beliefs are generalizations about our past based on our interpretations of painful and pleasurable experiences. It's not the events of our lives that shape us, but our beliefs as to what those events mean. It's never the events of our lives, but the meaning we attach to the events and how we interpret them. Beliefs are designed

117

to be a guiding force to tell us what will lead to pain and what will lead to pleasure. Beliefs play a major role in guiding our actions towards what would have, could have, and should have been. They help sustain us throughout our life." Tony Robbins.

GETTING THROUGH THE PAIN

Even though physical pain and emotional pain originate from the brain, I consider emotional pain the worse of the two. While in physical pain, your body throbs, aches, burns, and hurts from damaged tissue, but the pain leaves when the cause is cured. With emotional or mental pain, you relive previous experiences with seemingly no end in sight. For example, feeling desperate, alone, and empty may not be physical, but it can feel just as devastating as physical pain. In fact, it might be more harmful to you because it can turn into a physical ailment, such as back aches or fatigue, which no amount of drugs, food, sex, alcohol, or any other mind-deadening measure will heal.

Everyone experiences mental pain at some point in their life. It is not the pain itself, but our reaction to the pain that gives us the most grief. Often times I've asked myself "why, why am I going through this pain? What did I do to deserve this pain? Why am I so miserable? Am I that bad of a person? Is the reason I am in such pain my fault? Will my life be ruined because I am in such pain? Will I be able to overcome this pain?" These are only a few of the questions I have asked myself while going through the trauma of pain and I am sure you, the reader, have a few more "why" questions of your own.

I remember going through a painful time in my life when I could only find a single blade of grass to be grateful for or feel good about. I was sitting on a brick wall at work and feeling utterly miserable about my life when, all of a sudden, my eyes fell upon a single blade of grass. There must have been millions of blades of grass surrounding the brick wall, but only one caught my eye. While staring at the single blade of grass, my thoughts turned from feeling bad about my situation to marveling at the beauty of the blade of grass. After I picked it up, I twirled it through my fingers, admiring its shape, size, and color while smelling its fresh aroma. After holding it for a short time, I felt transported into a different realm of thinking. I was calmer and more focused, which helped me to cope and work through some issues.

I have spent numerous hours in self-talk fact finding which gave me a temporary moment of feeling empowered. Sure, I felt empowered while I was resolving an issue in my mind where I always came out on top of the situation, but that empowering feeling did not make a dent in the real reason for my mental distress, which sometimes became a noticeable physical pain. I would always wind up sighing to myself and with a heavy heart, repeating the words, "this too shall pass."

I never quite made peace with myself or felt truly happy before, during, or after my self-talk sessions. I was left with a continued yearning to be free from whatever was bothering me and had no way to completely heal from my yearning's clutches. While surfing on the Internet one day, I finally began to understand how deeply seated my negative emotions were. I had just completed another round of could have, should have, and would have and realized I was not helping myself heal the way I desperately wanted to. Suddenly, I heard the words "mustard seed". Remembering this as a parable from the Bible, I looked for a picture of a mustard seed. Once I saw how tiny it was, I began to take notice of my reaction to the picture before my eyes. Those words from the parable, "…….truly I tell you, if you have faith as small as a mustard seed, you can say to this mountain, 'Move from here to there,' and it will move. Nothing will be impossible for you.'" (Matthew 17:20)

The image of the tiny seed opened my mind to the possibility that through faith, all things are possible. I also became aware that if I wanted to be free of my emotional turmoil, I could be. Looking at the picture of the mustard seed and coming to the realization that I could finally be free from whatever emotional burdens I had been carrying felt like my being had been hit by a wakeup call. I stared at the mustard seed image without awareness of my surroundings for quite some time until the words mustard seed seemed to become a part of me. It was as if I had been redirected without any input from me to a different mental place. I now find looking at the picture of the mustard seed provides me with a different perspective. These days, when I face obstacles and fear tries to take over my thoughts, I pull out a picture of a mustard seed and remind myself to have faith because whatever I am experiencing has an expiration date.

RELEASING NEGATIVE EMOTIONS

When we suffer emotionally, we are experiencing negative emotional energy that has become trapped within us. Some signs of trapped emotional energy are when you experience sadness, despair, anger, fear, envy, dread, contempt, and annoyance, just to name a few. Emotions cause us to overreact by misinterpreting others' behavior, sabotage ourselves and our relationships, become physically ill, and they can lead to depression, anxiety, and ongoing, unshakeable, and unwanted feelings.

Could have, should have, and would have thoughts are the types of energies that force us to remain in pain. By getting rid of negative emotional thoughts, obstacles preventing us from moving into a positive state of mind are curtailed. To get rid of emotional thoughts, first choose to be free of them. Next, set your intention to remain in a peaceful state of mind. And last, each time a negative emotion enters your consciousness, change the thought to a positive one. You can do this by repeating a positive affirmation until the anxious feeling surrounding the emotion subsides. For instance, I am no longer a victim of this emotion. With the curtailment of negative emotions comes a renewed energy for life and we feel valuable, not only to others, but also to ourselves. When you set your intention to releasing negative emotions, you will become less and less overwhelmed by them. By consistently resolving to be free, you will become free. As for me, I refuse to hold on to guilt, shame, and dismay or remain a prisoner of negative emotions. How about you?

I HAVE NO HELP, OR DO I?

For those of you, like me, who find themselves in a position of not having a physical mentor or helper you can turn to, take heart. I have found that mentors or helpers come from a variety of sources. Whoever or whatever guides you in the direction you need to be in is a mentor or helper. I cannot count the times when I have been in need of some guidance and then find the answer on a magazine or book cover or just happen to turn to the exact TV channel I needed and the answer jumped out at me.

I found a mentor through the TV after lamenting about my inability to find a passionate avenue for my interest for the umpteenth time. For many years I have heard others say "search for your passion by digging deep inside, that is where your happiness lies". I was one of the people who never kept a passion. I learned a lot of things and had several businesses fail, but never quite felt like I was involved in an all-consuming endeavor. Whenever I thought about a life vocation, could have, should have, and would have interrupted any gains I made in finding the right fit for me. I would come up with an approach or idea I thought would work and then I would sabotage myself by thinking of all the ways it might not work.

This line of thinking rendered me useless and caused me to distrust my instincts in finding the right path. All this changed when I watched a recorded Oprah show, featuring Brene Brown. She told the story of how she had given a lecture and was feeling pretty good about herself until she read an email from one of the lecture attendees. The attendee advised Brene that thanks to her lecture, she had reached an all-time low point in her life because she had never been able, no matter how hard she tried, to find her passion. The attendee thanked Brene for making her feel so useless and hoped she had a good night's sleep. Brene implied she was caught off guard, but began to realize that the world needed people like the attendee. Brene termed the attendee "a humming bird" and talked about how the world needed humming birds. Brene reminded the listening audience that humming birds flew in various directions and helped to create harmony in the world. She went on to say there was nothing wrong with being a humming bird, that everyone was not cut out to charge about life, stubbornly engrossed in their passion, and that at some point, you would wind up exactly where you needed to be anyway.

I could not get that lecture out of my mind. The words "humming bird" rang true for my situation and me. I saw the correlation between the attendee and myself as the words humming bird reverberated in my head. I felt as though the attendee and I were kindred spirits and I no longer felt embarrassed not to be passionate about one set idea to the exclusion of everything else. It was a life changing experience for me and set me on the course of writing this book. On a happy note, could have, should have and would have no longer hold my interest and I am now preceding on a happy course of action, all because I found my mentor/helper by way of a television screen.

LONELINESS

"Loneliness is the leprosy of the modern world." Mother Theresa

If you feel lonely, you are feeling sad about being alone—been there plenty of times myself. Generally, most of us are social beings by our very nature and want some kind of positive attention from others. When we don't get enough of it, we feel deprived, causing us to feel lonely. Loneliness is a feeling you get when you feel unloved and it occurs whether you are in a crowd, with family or alone. It's one of those emotions that besets anyone at any time. It does not take into consideration your financial standing or expertise, your age, or even who you portray yourself to be. Loneliness can make you do things that you know are not in your best interests. An example of this is becoming involved with people who do not have your best interests at heart, simply because you feel you can't stand being by yourself one more minute.

To some, loneliness is the bane of their existence because it not only saps strength, but it can also take away the will to live. A lot of people commit suicide, take drugs, go on alcohol or food binges, or have a sexual marathon when the pain of loneliness becomes too great to bear. Here are a few suggestions when you are lonely: become passionate about something, stay busy, write in a journal, replace negative self-talk with gratitude for making it through each moment, or go to a store and start a conversation with another shopper (it can be about anything, i.e. this season's fashion colors, or the quality of fruits and vegetables).

JEALOUSY

"Envy is the art of counting another's blessing instead of your own." Harold Coffin.

In these paragraphs, I use envy and jealousy interchangeably. Envy is one of the most useless emotions one can experience. It does not serve you well and makes your life miserable because you are so intent on what another possesses that you forget about the goodness in your own life. You fixate on the qualities, achievements, or possessions of others, and you either desire what they have, or wish they didn't have it.

Having been down the road of envy a couple of times, I can tell you that road only served to make me miserable about my own life. The person(s) I was envious of kept right on achieving and living a wonderful life while I was left with yearning, contempt, anger, suspicion, and a host of could have, should have, and would have scenarios.

I was not a happy camper when I experienced jealousy. Then I learned a technique I want to share with you. Doing it immediately when I feel jealousy coming on takes me out of the emotional jealousy mode that pops up from time-to-time. Whenever you feel jealousy coming on, immediately stop. Briefly laugh, shake your head from side to side, and say to yourself, "God has been too good to me." If you like, you can also add, "to allow someone else's good to make me jealous." What this does is refocus your attention on your life and removes the emotional sabotage of jealousy. I call this my miracle technique because it works quickly and I am not left with any residual jealousy.

LESSONS OF LOVE

"Your task is not to seek for love, but merely to seek to find all the barriers with yourself that you have built against it." Rumi

I have talked about many things in the pages of this book surrounding feelings, except for my definition of love. Through experience, I have learned that when we are in a painful situation, we tend to forget there is a clarity about love that we have a hard time grasping due to the confusion our mind is experiencing at a given moment. I feel as though I would be leaving something undone if I did not discuss love's role in healing. I am not trying to redefine love. I only want to share my insights with you and perhaps give you another way to look at your perceptions about love. You may or may not agree with my definitions, and if not, please create a definition that gives your life purposeful meaning and one that works for you.

In order to realize that you are capable of love, you must first make a conscious choice to love. Do you choose to go about your life, steeped in self-absorbed thoughts about what's important to you only, while wanting someone to care about you? Or do you want to extend yourself beyond who you deem yourself to be and experience the joy and appreciation received from being cared about and caring about another? For instance, when a child is first born, we marvel at the tiny little being so dependent on us for survival. We entertain how great it feels and we relish the thought that we care so deeply about someone outside ourselves. We have chosen to love.

What is this thing called "forgiveness" and how do I do it? Forgiveness means you let go of the need to feel personal satisfaction for another individual receiving retribution. You release the need to think about hurting someone who has harmed you in some manner. You release your focus to wait for the downfall of another. You release the need to feel self-righteous indignation when you hear the offending person's name. You release any claim or hold on the welfare of someone who hurt you. While you may not understand why the person hurt you, you no longer allow yourself to be fueled by hatred for the individual. You allow yourself to remember that as a human being, everyone is prone to make mistakes so you forgive yourself and others by letting go of could have, should have, or would have thoughts.

Sometimes we dislike someone just because they appear in front of us. Sometimes we dislike someone for the harm they have heaped on us. We hold onto the emotion attached to our dislike and wear it as a badge of courage because we think it makes us strong. We may even hold onto an emotion we don't like because we want to keep the offending individual or situation at bay. We don't realize that, by rehashing old memories, we have kept the situation or person alive, thus enabling the situation or person to remain a part of our life. I bet you haven't realized that by holding onto the feeling of dislike for another, you continue to draw that type of individual into your life. Wayne Dyer, author, once wrote, "you can never get enough of what you don't want." Ever wonder why you keep repeating the same experience or meeting the same kind of person, even though you profess not to like the experience or person? The answer is you draw that type of individual or experience to you because you hold onto the memory of the experience. Notice how you react when the thought of the offender or experience pops into your mind. Do you rehash every nuance of the memory that caused you pain? When you hold onto a negative thought, feeling, or desire, you are destined to repeat whatever caused you angst, along with any negative emotion attached to it.

So how do you let go of dislike of another? Start by choosing. Choose to be free of the pain associated with the dislike. Choose to let go of the need to dislike. I have found if you carry around with you a dislike of something deep down inside, you feel as though you have a need to hold onto that dislike. Are you holding onto the dislike because you want to keep the offender at bay? Are you holding onto the dislike because it makes you feel stronger? Are you covering up some weakness? To be truly free of the associated pain carried with disliking, ask yourself why you are holding onto disliking something or someone, then make a conscious choice to let it go. Affirmations work wonders when trying to let go of bad choices. I discuss affirmations later in this book.

Sometimes we are forced to let go of something whether we want to or not. For instance, we are fired, not because of anything we have done, but because the company we worked for was downsized. At other times, we let go of something, for instance a dress we loved that once fit but is now two sizes too small, because we can no longer use it, or a relationship that felt right in the beginning, but later turned out to be a nuisance to maintain. There's an old saying, "when one door shuts another one will open". I believe this and have repeatedly experienced this adage first hand.

One particular time comes to mind when I went to visit a friend who lived about two hours away from my home. When I returned home, I found a charred heap being attended to by firemen. I was speechless, and stood staring incredulously at what once was my home, but was now a blackened heap of debris. I lost everything in that fire except the laundry I had previously placed in the trunk of my car to be laundered, the clothes on my back, and my car. I could have held on to the memory of what it felt like to lose most everything and continuously experienced the emotions associated with each lost item. I could have continuously talked about the fire in order to receive sympathy and remained in a pity party state of mind over what was lost in the fire, or I could have driven myself crazy, lamenting over what once was my home. I decided not to give into could have, should have, and would have which allowed me to embrace the new and not remain stuck and feeling powerless about things I had no control over. I did not feel cheated. I felt like I was given an opportunity to grow as a person. I started counting my blessings and found that a deeper level of faith had entered my consciousness. I felt as though I had found a part of me that I did not know existed. What I gained from the loss of my home was a new perspective of life and a sense of purpose.

One final word about letting go. If you feel stuck in a place you don't want to be, such as a painful relationship, ask yourself why you find it necessary to remain where you hurt? Do you want or need to continue reeling from the pain of being associated with something or someone you have outgrown? Are you holding onto something because you feel you have no other out? Are you holding on because you have carried the pain for so long that it seems to be a part of you? Have you pushed pain deeper inside yourself each time someone comes back into your life because they are related to you by blood and they profess to need your help?

If you can answer "yes" to any of these questions, ask yourself why you find it necessary to remain in a hurtful place. Then ask yourself if it is worth the pain. You can start healing from a hurtful place by counting your blessings (count everything before your eyes that you have accumulated as a blessing—because it is). Feel grateful for your five senses (this may take a concerted effort on your part if you are near despair, but keep trying and the feeling will come). Recognize you can feel grateful for reminding yourself that you have value and are valuable (feeling grateful doesn't have to be about big things in your life because everything you have is a blessing).,

Have you ever come into contact with a person who continuously boasts about their personal life? I have. After a while, I shun that person every time I see them because I get tired of hearing about their supposedly well-adjusted, bountiful life. I am not talking about the person who has achieved their dreams and is using their life as a model to help others achieve goals. I am talking about the braggart whose life is too good to be true. The person who says they never experience ups or downs or who says they always comes out on top, a person who displays a "holier than thou" attitude. Anyone displaying these types of behaviors is not coming from a loving part of themselves. They are coming from fear-based emotions. Love exists in quietness. It does not have to be seen to be felt. It does not ask to be given something in order to receive something. Love gives without thought of "what's in it for me". You can count on love to support and nurture you. Love will never say "I give you something so you must give me something in return". Love does not boast in any way about helping you. If you run across someone displaying boastful tendencies, don't be fooled by their charm, good looks, or supposedly good life. See them as the scared person they really are and, for your own sake, do not get sucked into the web of falsities they portray.

Love gives from that deep place inside you where no one else resides, without thought of "what's in it for me". Love does not do something for someone else while expecting something in return. Have you ever asked a person whom you thought was a friend for a favor, have that person grant you the favor, and then demand you do something for them in return? I have only met this type of person a few times, but when I did meet them, I have been very sorry for asking help from them. Usually, the lesson learned from an exchange with this type of individual teaches us to refrain from asking for favors, even when we really need help, because we may not be in a position or want to pay back a favor. Sometimes if we are unable to return a favor, the person owed the favor may resort to coercion or try to make us feel guilty in order to get what they want. The gratitude felt by the person who received the favor then turns into resentment for being placed in a position of feeling guilty. This kind of interchange usually leads to hard feelings between both parties. A person coercing you to do something does not have your best interests at heart no matter how much they sugarcoat their request. The best solution I know is to cut off all association with the coercer and ask God to bless them, because not one person who loves you will coercively ask you to do something.

I often come into contact with some who are so down on themselves I wonder how they get through a day. Their view of the world seems filled with anger, fear, distrust, and a generally negative way of looking at everything. I get as far away from this type of individual as fast as I can while reminding myself that love is kind and gentle. To me, this person carries so much negative energy that it is very difficult to have a conversation with them. No matter how much I try to reach this person, they only want to dwell on the negative aspects of life. Even though I believe we are, or can be, our brother's keeper, I also believe we cannot help someone who is not ready to be helped. And, in order to preserve my own sanity and not get sucked into the negative person's world, I run for my life in the opposite direction as far away from them as possible.

My observation of this type of individual has taught me that I need to commit to loving myself with all of my might, that no one who walks this earth can love me better than I can love myself, that loving myself means being kind to myself in every way, and that calling myself unkind names, such as stupid or the "B" word, is being disrespectful and creating a self-made victim mentality within me. Now when I find myself being unloving and calling myself names like stupid or the "B" word, I stop immediately and think of a kind, nice thing to say to myself even if I have to repeat something that someone has previously said to me. I now understand the more I can realize I am worthy of love, the more loving people I encounter. A side benefit of being kind and nurturing to one's self is that you come into your own personal power and do not allow anyone who is not loving towards you to remain in your personal space.

MOVING ON

Holding onto unresolved emotional turmoil is like walking around with a severely injured foot that is encased in a heavy medical boot. You know the open-toed, full leg, micro-fastened, heavy boot you get from a doctor or a hospital after you have been hurt. The injured foot is representative of the pain you keep buried inside and the medical boot is representative of the ways and means you use to hide the pain. The medical boot keeps your foot stationary and makes the foot feel secure and uninjured. That is, until your foot missteps, someone steps on your toes, or you fall. Then the excruciating pain reminds you that your foot has been hurt. In order for your foot to heal, you have to do certain things: rest, put ice on it, and elevate it above your heart. It takes a while for it to heal, but it does heal.

Moving on from hurt, pain, shame, and guilt are accomplished in much the same manner. You forgive (put ice on it), let go of the offense (rest), and choose love over negative emotions (elevate your foot above your heart.)

YOU NEVER GET ENOUGH OF WHAT YOU DON'T WANT

"You can't get enough of what you don't want" is a phrase coined by Dr. Wayne Dyer. I am sometimes reminded of the power of this statement whenever I rehash a memory. Think about it: a memory shows up that you are really tired of or haven't healed from yet and sets into motion all the emotions that make you feel guilty, ashamed, sad, angry, or frustrated. You recognize this memory as the harbinger of bad feelings and you may even fight with yourself to be free of its hold on you. Did you notice how the memory returns again and again even though you don't want it to? This is what is meant by never getting enough of what you don't want. It's just like when you wish to find something, a job, new career, new adventure, or your keys, and the very thing you wish for shows up. So it goes with what you don't want. Because you consistently dwell on the memory and its attendant emotion, the memory shows up in your life in ways you don't wish to continue to experience. Another example is when you keep repeating the same situations with the same type of person, including the events and circumstances that arose from the situation, because you continually dwell, either consciously or sub-consciously, on the very thing you wish to be free of. This type of attraction can go on for quite some time unless you make a concerted effort to heal or get at the root cause of your distress.

MAKE A CHOICE, YOU WON'T BE SORRY

The operative thought in this book is, *you must choose.* Choose who you are, choose your values and beliefs, choose when to say no, choose to be or not to be a victim, choose to let go of everyone who mistreats you in any way. Maya Angelou once wrote, "when a person shows you who they are, believe them." Too many times we choose to make excuses for the offending person, who may even be a person we have sacrificed for. A lot of times, we feel as though we are indebted to an individual because they are the result of our procreation efforts. We may also feel indebted to someone who has helped us in some way in the past. When we don't choose, we allow ourselves to be placed in the position of being victimized. So choose, choose to be free of this kind of emotional garbage. Then set your intentions to living in a peaceful state of mind. Remember, only you can choose when enough is enough and make the kinds of changes that will enhance your life and allow you to be free of inner turmoil.

A Countryman's son by accident trod upon a Serpent's tail, which turned and bit him so that he died. The father in a rage got his axe, and pursuing the Serpent, cut off part of its tail. So the Serpent in revenge began stinging several of the Farmer's cattle and caused him severe loss. Well, the Farmer thought it best to make it up with the Serpent, and brought food and honey to the mouth of its lair, and said to it: "Let's forget and forgive; perhaps you were right to punish my son, and take vengeance on my cattle, but surely I was right in trying to revenge him; now that we are both satisfied why should not we be friends again?" "No, no," said the Serpent; "take away your gifts; you can never forget the death of your son, nor I the loss of my tail." Injuries may be forgiven, but not forgotten. Aesop Fables, The Man and the Serpent

One of the best lessons I have ever learned is that forgiveness means letting go. You don't have to forget what happened, but you don't have to dwell on it either. You forgive the person for your sake because forgiveness is for you, not the other person. The other person can take care of themselves.

LEARNING TO FORGIVE

When we are in the throes of inner conflict between our need to feel anger or resentment and our need for inner peace, we are bombarded with all the reasons we cannot let go of our requisite to feel right about being wronged in some manner. We self-righteously assert our need to feel anger or resentment. We want retribution for our pain and feel a surge of power within us that allows us to feel powerful and self-assertive. We may lose all manner of reason if we have reached a point in our anger in which we have no other thoughts except the eradication of the offender. We may even give in to our need to strike back at the offender by hurting or harming them in some way. We will feel gleeful if we find the offending party is having difficulty in their life because we believe they are receiving their 'just reward'. Sometimes our anger towards another continues even after the person who offended us has died. We become so steeped in the emotional trappings of feeling offended that we hang onto the emotion in order to lessen our inner pain. Alexander Pope, English poet, wrote, "to err is human, to forgive, divine." What we don't realize is that we carry an unnecessary burden when we fail to forgive another. The ironic part of non-forgiveness is that we want and expect to be forgiven of our transgressions, yet we may fail to forgive another of theirs. My guardian used to say, "child, if you are mad at somebody, I am mad at them, too." This never made sense to me. As a child, I wondered why we could not just let go of the offense and be friends with the offender. I did not understand at the time that I was beginning to define forgiveness.

132

What is forgiveness? Forgiveness means that you stop feeling angry or resentful toward someone for an offense, flaw, or mistake. Forgiveness does not mean you forget an offense; it means you refuse to carry the burden of rehashing your angst about it. Forgiveness allows you to live your life comfortably. What do I mean by this? I mean you can live your life free of the need to walk around as a wounded victim because someone hurt or neglected you. You can live free of all guilt or shame. How much better would you feel if you did not have to carry around negative emotions that have been generated by negative thought? I can tell you from personal experience, when you have forgiven someone, a heaviness you did not know you felt departs from you and your whole being feels light. You experience true happiness that emanates from within. You feel peaceful. You no longer feel anger or resentment, which frees up space within you that you can fill with compassion and love. Your attitude changes from feeling sorry for yourself to gratitude for what you have and for what you have accomplished in life. You feel alive, and best of all, you forgive yourself for any missteps you have made. You begin to look at the world in a different way, as if seeing it for the very first time. You aspire to be more of the new you and you begin to see the world as a place of possibilities instead of more of the same old stink, but different toilet.

If you want to be free of a pain-causing memory, set your intention to forgive the offender and let the experience go by repeating, "I forgive you (fill in the blank)" until you feel better. It may take a while because your emotions may be deeply rooted, but if you keep at it, you will forgive the person or let go of the event and could have, should have, and would have will no longer present a problem in connection with that particular issue.

BEING ALONE DOES NOT MEAN LONELINESS

When my youngest child went off to experience his own life, I was left with a blank space in mine. I was alone and felt at odds with everything that existed in my world. Whenever I looked into the room where he normally slept, I felt desolate and lonely. Instead of cooking for one person, I prepared meals for at least two, so I wasted a lot of food. Having no one to talk to at home, except four walls, made me feel as though the house was pushing in on me. I felt as though I didn't have a purpose for working anymore.

My emotional downslide changed when I came home from work one day, sat on the sofa, and began to stare out the patio door. Looking at my backyard, it suddenly dawned on me that this was now my life and I had a choice to make. I could either continue on a path of feeling alone and discombobulated or I could create a life for myself by learning new things and adjusting to a new way of living. Needless to say, I chose the latter because I realized I could dream dreams that were for me alone, I could enhance my life through learning new skills. I no longer had the responsibility of being the watchdog of another and I could establish a life just for me.

With these revelations came a feeling of relief and euphoria because now, for the first time in my life, I only had to answer to me and I could begin to do so immediately. What I learned from this experience is that being alone is a perfect growth opportunity time. And I realized that feeling alienated from others as a child helped to mold me into a person who could be alone without feeling lonely.

ALTERNATIVE HEALING METHODS

EFT/TAPPING

One of the surest ways I have found helpful in dealing with emotional problems brought on by would have, could have, and should have is called the "emotional flooding technique" (EFT), also known as tapping. EFT is useful in helping overcome emotional, and sometimes physical pain, by targeting the root cause of the pain you are experiencing. It does this by quickly interrupting the body's stress responses through touch. I won't go into the intricacies of tapping here because there is quite a bit of material on the market that describes how to do tapping and the benefits from tapping.

This technique, though simple, is very effective in overcoming emotional dis-ease. I first came across EFT on the Internet while looking for an alternative method to medication. I was stressed and felt as though my life was taking me in a direction I did not want to go. When I first found EFT, I did not believe something so simple could be so effective, but decided to try it anyway. To my amazement, my stress level decreased considerably and the issues I was stressed about melted away each time I practiced EFT. The more I practiced it, the more in touch I became with my own true feelings, and once I recognized the cause of the issues surrounding my feelings, the issues resolved themselves.

Not only did I help myself, but I also was able to help a neighbor by using EFT. During an annual Christmas dinner, I ran into a neighbor who sat off to himself and looked as though he was in great pain. After saying hello, I asked him what was going on with him. I knew he had lost his son a couple months before so I thought he was undergoing the emotional pain of losing a loved one. To my surprise, he told me he was ready to commit suicide. Normally I feel if you are depressed enough to want to take your life, I am of no help to you. But for some reason, I cannot explain, I asked him to come to see me so I could help him. I did not know exactly how to help him other than to let him grieve about his son by talking about the loss. I figured this would be a good time to use EFT. When he came over, I allowed him to express his pain for a short while, and then broached the subject of EFT with him. He agreed to try it and I took him through an EFT session. After the session, he not only looked less depressed, but also expressed how much better he felt and how he no longer wished to commit suicide. After his second visit with me, he talked about how much he had improved and how he was now able to drive past his son's residence, which was something he couldn't do before. After the third visit, he was able to use EFT to help himself continue to heal. Helping him gave me an even greater appreciation of the effectiveness of EFT so I am sharing this technique with you. You can find out more information about EFT/tapping at www.tapping.com.

MEDITATION

Before I understood meditation, I used to pooh, pooh it. I thought it was something regimented and it seemed every book I read on the subject had a different way of doing a systematic routine. It became a total "turn off" for me and I was not about to put myself through a routine that seemed farfetched, anyway. I also thought it seemed complicated and time consuming. I have since learned meditation is a restful, get-to-the-core-of-a-problem, self-sustaining way of receiving help. When I first learned how to meditate, various thoughts interrupted my session and I felt as though it was useless to even try any kind of meditative technique.

Okay, here's what I now know about meditation. The purpose of meditation is to assist one in bringing about the peaceful solution to inner turmoil and to help one enjoy a sense of well-being while engaging in life activities. Did you know that you have meditated even though you did not realize you were doing it? I didn't at first. If you are in deep thought about something and are unaware of your surroundings, you are meditating. There is no set way to meditate because anytime you are engaged in deep concentration, you are in a meditative state.

The routine I now use to meditate is to turn off all electronics and sit in a spot away from my cell phone. I don't worry about thoughts interrupting my session. Instead, I think of or remind myself of the issues I need answers for. Next, I either place my hands comfortably in my lap or place my thumb against my index finger. I then take a deep breath in and slowly release the breath. My next step is to focus my attention on the slow intake of my breath and the slow release of my breath. I do this until I feel I have sat long enough or gotten answers to my questions—usually ten to forty-five minutes. You won't always receive an answer to your question during a meditation session, but you will get an answer, and sometimes from unexpected places or strangers. My only caution concerns the onslaught of thoughts that try and impede your progress. Don't fight the thought. I repeat, don't fight the thought— just notice the thought and let it go on its merry way. Your thoughts may entice you to do something other than meditate by reminding you of what you haven't gotten done, such as your laundry, making up your grocery list, things you forgot to do, or left undone. Don't pay attention. Don't fight with the thought, just let it say whatever it wants to say, and return to focusing on your breathing. You may feel like your thoughts are winning, but I can assure you that once your mind accepts that, you will meditate regardless of the messages it is sending to you. It will cease to bother you for the most part with thoughts when you are meditating.

ACUPRESSURE

Acupressure is similar to acupuncture and also touches some of the same areas as massage. The difference between acupressure and acupuncture is that acupressure does not use needles and is easy to learn, whereas acupuncture requires extensive study and uses what I call an instrument that can turn a strong man weak: a needle. I find acupressure most helpful when I need instant relief from pain I'm experiencing in my body. Not only does it help the physical pain, but it also helps any mental pain, by interrupting the body's response to pain. This helps me settle down because the stress of feeling pain is gone. You can find loads of tips on acupressure at www.acupressure.com.

AFFIRMATIONS

Affirmations are one of my favorite "go to" tools when I feel out of sorts. I learned about affirmations because it literally jumped out at me while browsing a bookstore. I thought of its public proponent, Louise Hay, as a mentor for quite some time. I still refer to her as the "affirmation guru" who helped me get rid of some pain by refocusing my attention to a more positive approach to problem solving. While affirmations can take a while depending on how deeply ingrained the cause of your pain is, I found that pain diminishes within a reasonably short time, and before very long, I reaped the benefit of emotional freedom. I highly recommend you take a look at Louise Hay's website at www.louisehay.com.

RECAP OF LESSONS LEARNED ALONG THE WAY

Fear: Allowing fear to place and hold you in a vice-like grip is akin to allowing your life to stagnate to the point of uselessness. We will always have to contend with fear, but it does not have to immobilize us into inaction. Whenever you feel uncontrollably fearful, look around your home and, out loud, thank God for everything he has given you right down to the minutest object in your possession. You can also recite the two definitions of fear as a reminder to not allow fear to rule your life: "forget everything and run, or face everything and rise. The choice is yours," author unknown.

Gratitude: One of the most beneficial healing methods I have found involves gratitude. Put a stop to negative emotions that latch on to you and won't let go by being grateful for what you have and what you have accomplished. Replace negative self-talk with gratitude. Look around and say out loud, or in silence, "I am grateful for (fill in the blank)". Everything before your eyes that belongs to you is something to be grateful for.

Jealousy/envy: Being jealous or envious of someone else's good is a choice, and a miserable one at that. To combat jealousy/envy, briefly laugh, shake your head from side to side, and say to yourself, "God has been too good to me." This will refocus your attention on your life and remove the emotional sabotage of jealousy.

Self-victim: Becoming a victim of your own emotions and to circumstances beyond your control depletes your internal strength. If you allow yourself to become self-victimized or victimized by others, you give your negative emotions and others free rein to control every aspect of your life. In order to remain in control of who we are, we must choose to be or not to be a victim. Choose who we are. Choose our values and beliefs. Choose when to say no. Choose to let go of everyone who mistreats us in any way. In other words, we must set personal boundaries. When we don't set boundaries, we allow ourselves to be placed in the position of being victimized.

Seesaw/Crazy eight pattern: When you experience the seesaw or crazy eight pattern, you experience two emotions in direct opposition to each other, taking turns activating and releasing each other. Such as anger and frustration being replaced with helplessness and sadness. To stop this type of pattern, start a healing process. Meditate, pray, go for a walk, look for things around you to be grateful for, use EFT, acupressure, or any of the many healing disciplines available for you to discover

Guilt and shame: Moving on from hurt, pain, shame, and guilt are accomplished by forgiveness, letting go of the offense, and choosing to love rather than experience a negative emotion.

Letting go of another: To let go of another means to release another through forgiveness. If you have hit a brick wall in your relationship with another and can find no way to have peaceful exchanges with the individual, set your intention to living free from the pain you are experiencing. Once you have set your intention to live free from pain, begin to let go of the need to be needed by someone who is deliberately hurting you. Let go of the sorrow you feel because you can't have or don't have a relationship with someone. If a person is meant to be in your life, they will be.

Rejection: Not someone's "cup of tea?" It's okay. Remember you are important, and by virtue of you're being here on earth, have value. Just because the person doesn't like you, does not mean they are not a nice person or can be a friend to someone else. To release the emotional turmoil of rejection, try affirmations as a way of getting to the root cause of your pain. Doing affirmation exercises helps to keep you balanced, and life can take on new meaning.

Loneliness: Loneliness, is that dreaded time in life when we wish we were anywhere other than where we find ourselves at the moment. To some, loneliness is so painful, it leaves little room for anything else. If you experience this type of loneliness, allow yourself to reconnect with your inner being by briefly experiencing the loneliness without fighting to control it. If you don't acknowledge that you are lonely by allowing yourself to temporarily experience it, you allow it to fester and become a part of your personality. After you connect with your inner being, immediately turn your attention to something that can take your mind off of the loneliness, such as a computer game. Here are a few additional suggestions to help when you find you are lonely: become passionate about something, stay busy, write in a journal, replace negative self-talk with gratitude for making it through each moment, or go to a store and start a conversation with another shopper (it can be about anything, i.e. this season's fashion colors, or the quality of fruits and vegetables).

Releasing negative emotions: A line from a song by En Vogue says, "free your mind and the rest will follow." This line could have been written for negative emotions. Once you stop allowing a negative emotion to run your life, obstacles preventing you from moving into a positive state of mind are curtailed. To get rid of negative emotional thoughts, first choose to be free of them. Next, set your intention to remain in a peaceful state of mind. And last, each time a negative emotion enters your consciousness, change the thought to a positive one. You can do this by repeating a positive affirmation until the anxious feeling surrounding the emotion subsides. For instance, "I am no longer a victim of this emotion".

Pain: Remember, pain has an expiration date. What this means is that every painful circumstance or situation that is a part of your life today will end at some point in time. It does not matter whether the ending is through rejection, abandonment, death, or you leave the painful place, an end will come.

A better frame of mind: To change to a better frame of mind, find something that encourages you to feel better. It does not have to be something as grand as a shopping trip or new love interest. It can be a kind word, a picture of a time when you felt at peace, or just look around you and rediscover all the things you have been blessed with, and feel the gratitude of having these things.

Set your intention to finding the cause of your distress: This may take a moment because we are not always clear about the cause of our pain, but your intention to understand the real reason why you hurt will go a long way to getting at the root of your pain. For quite a bit of my life, it has been difficult to understand the underlying reason for any pain I experienced. I've come to understand how hard it is to accept that emotions, such as anger and jealousy, that you refuse to let go of as well as other unresolved trauma become so deeply rooted within you they become a part of your personality. They get locked in to who you are. Add in some outdated beliefs and you'll find most of the culprits responsible for making you unnecessarily miserable.

See your adult child as an adult human being who is now operating on his or her own mores and values: No matter how hard you may have worked to instill great values in your child, the bottom line is he/she will live according to what he/she deems appropriate for his/her existence.

Believe, really believe, that you can live without could have, should have, and would have thoughts, because you can: In the beginning, it takes practice to catch yourself in the process of returning to old habits, but with consistent practice, it becomes second nature. You will always reinforce negative emotions, such as anger, frustration, regret, fear, shame, guilt, sadness, self-pity, just to name a few, when you repeat them, and by repeating negative emotions, you make them a part of your personality.

A FINAL NOTE

"What we know matters, but who we are matters more." Author unknown.

It is my desire and fervent wish that by revealing my story, my outlook on life and the things I have learned along the way, you who read this book will know and appreciate the lovely spirit you are. I hope you will be able to leave behind the guilt and shame associated with could have, should have, and would have. I recognize there are times in our lives when we feel completely alone, rejected, abandoned, angry, sad, and in such inner turmoil, that it is hard to comprehend we are not the only person experiencing a tumultuous situation. I would like you to remember you are never the only one experiencing a difficult time. Everyone has peaks and valleys, rough roads and smooth roads. No one escapes, absolutely no one. Even if the experience is not quite the same as another's, we all, every one that walks this earth, experience the same emotions. It took a lot of years for me to recognize I am not alone in any difficulty and to understand that focusing on what is happening instead of what I want to happen, is only conducive to bringing more of what I don't want.

Often we fret over bygone experiences and continue to live in the past by daily focusing on what transpired in the past. We cry over the way things might have been, if only this or that had happened. We fail to realize that our true nature has been hidden amongst our desire to make things the way we want them to be. Our quest for reliving what could have happened, should have happened and would have happened diametrically opposes our reality of the here and now. We continue to hurt because it feels too difficult to let go of what no longer has value. Because we are afraid of the future, we remain a part of our past. We often allow our past decisions to override any gains we might make if we were to move forward, away from how things could have been, into a new vision of how things can be.

Mental pain can permeate every one of our thoughts and actions. It takes no mercy, and can define how you react to life in general if you let it. When you allow mental pain to run rampant in your life, your old buddies, could have, should have, and would have come knocking on your door, causing you to further spiral down the paths of shame and guilt. You then re-experience the seesaw/crazy eight pattern of feeling sad until you get tired of sadness and move on to anger until your body gets tired of that. Then you go back to sadness, and so on, until you may feel as though you are about to go crazy or drown in your own emotions.

Making a change in how we think can appear to be a daunting task. Many "how to" books have been written proclaiming to have a surefire way to get on with life. The only surefire way I know of starts by first wanting to make a change in your life. Next, and watch out for this one, pay attention to how the necessary things you need to make the change show up. It's as if a new world opens up for you in alignment with your desire for change, and in one form or another, it sends you exactly what you need at just the right time from just the right source. I am always amazed at the perfect timing of my needs being met.

I have come to realize that, when you understand the reason behind any pain you experience, you are able to decide how to respond to an experience. While it may seem hard to believe, pain is one of the best pathways to healing. I am not advocating pain. I'm saying that it is a good instrument for self-discovery, because most time, the only way you can make a decision to change your life is when you are in a painful state.

Remember, use memories, but do not allow memories to use you. If a memory makes you feel bad, start a healing process. Meditate, pray, go for a walk, look for things around you to be grateful for, use EFT, acupressure, or any of the many healing disciplines available for you to discover. If a memory allows you to experience it as a growth tool, then it is a good memory and can be thoroughly investigated and used for your good.

In closing, I wish you love and peaceful solutions to all your life challenges. May you receive all the blessings that your heart and hands can hold.

ABOUT ARTRELLA

After serving in the U.S. Army Reserves and retiring from federal government service, Artrella Mack now dedicates herself full-time to supporting others in their search for self-realization. She is an emotional freedom techniques (EFT) and an acupressure advisor who demonstrates to others, by example, that they can heal the emotional trauma generated by repeatedly reliving past mistakes through the lenses of shame and guilt. Artrella is an artist, lecturer, teacher and business owner with a master's degree in business administration, and can be reached through her website: http://www.artrella.org.

Made in the USA
Charleston, SC
12 December 2016